THE PHILOSOPHY OF ALEXANDER CAMPBELL

A Bethany College Benedum Foundation Regional American
Studies Publication

The Philosophy of Alexander Campbell, by S. Morris Eames

THE PHILOSOPHY OF ALEXANDER CAMPBELL

by

S. Morris Eames

Southern Illinois University

Foreword

by

Perry E. Gresham

President of Bethany College

A Comprehensive Bibliography of Alexander Campbell's Writings

by

Claude E. Spencer

Curator Emeritus, Disciples of Christ Historical Society

Bethany, West Virginia:
BETHANY COLLEGE

Printed by Standard Press, New Brunswick, New Jersey

To the Memory of

HENRY BARTON ROBISON

Beloved Teacher and Friend

CONTENTS

FOREWORD

Alexander Campbell deserves a place of honor in West Virginia's hall of fame along with Abraham Lincoln. Campbell won the political contest which sent him to the Virginia Constitutional Convention in 1829 where he debated the mighty heroes of the Old Dominion — Madison, Monroe, Marshall, and Randolph. The rift between the slaveholding East and the abolitionist West appeared at that historic convention in the "King Numbers" address of Mr. Campbell. Thirty-four years later the state was divided by Lincoln's proclamation. Archibald Campbell, nephew of Alexander, called the convention which founded West Virginia.

A visitor to Utah will meet with the Mormons everywhere. A visitor to West Virginia, however, must have a dedication to research if he discovers that the religious body known variously as the Christian Churches, the Disciples of Christ, The Churches of Christ, The Restoration Movement, and the Campbellites originated in the home of Alexander Campbell at Bethany. Bethany College, founded in 1840, was built on Campbell's farm with Campbell's money. The institution was a college of arts and sciences from the outset with a self-perpetuating Board of Trustees and the curious provision that no professorship of theology should ever be established.

Dr. S. Morris Eames writes this volume with double competence as a disciplined philosopher and as an expert on Alexander Campbell. Campbell's complicated thought is systematically set forth with sympathy, perceptivity, and critical candor. Bethany College is honored to publish the volume as part of its American Studies program supported by the Claude Worthington Benedum Foundation and the Oreon E. Scott Foundation. Vachel Lindsay, an Illinois poet who viewed Campbell as a philosopher hero, spoke the appropriate word for *The Philosophy of Alexander Campbell* by S. Morris Eames when he wrote:

> Let a thousand Prophets have their due
> Let each have his boat in the sky
> But you were born for his secular millennium
> With the old Kentucky forest blooming like heaven,
> And the redbirds flying high.

Perry E. Gresham, President
Bethany College
Bethany, West Virginia

9

PREFACE

On April 26 and 27, 1965, I gave the Oreon E. Scott lectures at Bethany College, Bethany, West Virginia. The lectures were warmly received and I was asked to make them available in book form. In order to round out a comprehensive presentation of Alexander Campbell's principal ideas, I have added a chapter on his ethics, politics, and education; I have written an introductory chapter on Campbell's significance and a concluding chapter on his legacy.

I hope that the readers of this work will keep in mind that these chapters were first presented in lecture form, thus I have tried to keep the mechanics of footnoting at a minimum. I have tried to make references only to the central and crucial passages in Campbell's writings. This presentation of Campbell's philosophy and religion is intended as an introductory exposition and interpretation of his thought.

During my visit at Bethany College, I was graciously entertained by President and Mrs. Perry E. Gresham. I had the opportunity to discuss the contents of the lectures with others who appeared on the program. I learned much from these discussions and I have been influenced by some of these criticisms which I have woven into the final draft of the book. Among those with whom these discussions were especially enlightening are: Professors James W. Carty, Jr., Harold Dosten, Richard B. Kenney, Jefferson Hamilton, Robert Myers, Robert A. Preston, and Farrell D. Walters. I was pleased to appear on the programs with Leroy Garrett, Professor of Philosophy, Texas Women's University. I learned many things from Professor Garrett, and I appreciate deeply the kindly way in which he approaches the problem of the fragmentation of the church in the contemporary world.

My understanding of the thought of Alexander Campbell has been deepened and broadened by the many excellent works which have appeared in recent years. Among these should be mentioned the following: Robert Frederick West, *Alexander Campbell and Natural Religion* (New Haven: Yale University Press, 1948); the books published by Bethany Press, St. Louis, Missouri, are of great value to any student of Alexander Campbell's life and thought: Harold L. Lunger, *The Political Ethics of Alexander Campbell*, 1954; Granville T. Walker, *Preaching in the Thought of Alexander Campbell*, 1954; D. Ray Lindley, *Apostle of Freedom*, 1957; Cecil K. Thomas, *Alexander Campbell and His New Version*, 1958; Oliver

Read Whitley, *Trumphet Call of Reformation,* 1959; Royal Humbert, *Compend of Alexander Campbell's Theology,* 1961. One of the most valuable books in evaluating the significance of Alexander Campbell, also published by Bethany Press, is *The Sage of Bethany: A Pioneer in Broadcloth,* 1960, compiled by Perry E. Gresham. The essays compiled in this volume are first-rate and the number of scholars impressive: President Gresham, Arthur Schlesinger, Jr., Winfred E. Garrison, Louis Cochran, Roland Bainton, Stephen J. England, Harold L. Lunger, and Eva Jean Wrather. The many books written by Winfred Ernest Garrison must be singled out as an example of excellent scholarship and insight; among these I would like to mention his work, *The Sources of Alexander Campbell's Theology* (St. Louis: Christian Publishing Co., 1900). Dr. Garrison's work was one of the first I read on this phase of Campbell's thought and my indebtedness to him is extensive.

I owe much to the late J. William Hudson, Lathrop Professor of Philosophy, University of Missouri, who first suggested that I write a book on Campbell's philosophy and religion. My former teachers and present colleagues, Professors Willis Moore and Lewis E. Hahn, have constantly encouraged me in my research.

President Gresham graciously agreed to write the Foreword to the book. I am indebted to Dr. Claude E. Spencer, curator emeritus of the Disciples of Christ Historical Society, Nashville, Tennessee, who has allowed me to append his comprehensive bibliography of Campbell's writings to the volume. Dr. Spencer's contribution to my work is an example of his capable scholarship and of his devotion of many years to the preservation of the history and literature of the Disciples of Christ.

I am grateful to Mr. Darryl Brown and to Mrs. Polly V. Dunn who helped with the preparation of the manuscript. Throughout the preparation of the lectures and the re-working of the manuscript, I was given constant and valuable aid by my wife, Elizabeth Ramsden Eames. While many people aided me in the entire task, whatever errors of fact and of interpretation may be found in the book are my own responsibility.

The book is dedicated to the late Henry Barton Robison, beloved teacher and friend, whose influence upon me has been so extensive that it cannot be measured.

S. M. E.

Lake Muskoka, Ontario
September, 1966

I

THE SIGNIFICANCE OF ALEXANDER CAMPBELL

Alexander Campbell was one of the founders and the most influential leader of the largest group of Christian people which had its origin upon American soil. In many respects this religious leader stood far ahead of many of his contemporaries in intellectual matters, in matters touching upon philosophy, religion, science, morals, politics, and education. Campbell had a purpose and a plan through which he sought to heal the divisions within Christendom. This program stemmed from his sensitivity to the pressing problems of his age and from an intellectual capacity to put forth ideas which could stand the test of criticism and which would be plausible and appealing to the minds of the people to whom they were addressed.

The span of years from 1788, when Alexander Campbell was born, to 1866, when he died, was a period when the revolutions begun in the sixteenth and seventeenth centuries were working their way to fulfillment in the Western world. Copernicus had turned men's minds away from the earth as the center of things and started them searching the heavens for new truths. Francis Bacon had attacked the old methods of knowing of Scholasticism and had pleaded with men to open their eyes to the observations they could make of nature. Martin Luther had challenged the hierarchy of authority in religious institutions and had let loose in the world a new psychological and social freedom with the philosophy that every man is his own priest. Sir Isaac Newton had shown man what a marvelously ordered universe he lives in and had made this order the work of God. These revolutionary movements in science, philosophy, and religion came to a more complete fulfillment in the eighteenth century, and the new ideas received a more mature statement, a clearer and fuller expression, in writers such as John Locke.

Campbell spent most of the early part of his life in Ireland, some of it in Scotland, where he was educated in the prevailing philosophies and religious ideas of his time. [1] His father, Thomas Campbell, a sensitive and well trained minister, had attended the University of Glasgow. Under the guidance of his father, Alexander Campbell had read Locke's *Essay Concerning Human Understanding*

---

[1] For a rich source of information concerning Alexander Campbell's life, see Robert Richardson, *Memoirs of Alexander Campbell* (Cincinnati: Standard Publishing Co., 1913), Vols. I and II.

and the *Letters on Toleration* early in his life. Because of his health, Thomas Campbell was compelled to leave Ireland in 1807, and he made his new home in the United States, migrating finally to the western part of Pennsylvania. The family remained in Ireland until arrangements could be made to bring them to the new country. In September, 1808, the Campbell family started on their voyage. Because of a storm in which their ship was wrecked off the coast of Scotland, the group was detained about a year. During this time the Campbell family resided in Glasgow and Alexander took the opportunity to study at the university. In 1809, Alexander Campbell finally arrived in the United States.

While at the University of Glasgow, Campbell deepened his knowledge of the Scottish Common-sense school of philosophy. The principal leaders of this school of thought were Thomas Reid and Dugald Stewart. Thomas Reid had retired from his chair only a few years before Thomas Campbell, Alexander's principal tutor, attended there. But Reid's influence was still dominant when both of the Campbells studied in Glasgow. Alexander studied Greek, Latin, and French; more important contributions to his later development, however, were the courses he took in logic and experimental philosophy. He also read James Beattie's *Ethics* and Mackenzie's *Man of Feeling.* These studies left a lasting impression upon his mind, and his own philosophy and religion draws upon these and many other sources in the construction of his principal ideas.

On the religious side of his experience, Campbell had been reared in the Seceder branch of the Presbyterian church in which his father was a minister. The county of Antrim, Ireland, where Alexander was born, had been settled by Scotch immigrants who had been lured there with economic promises made by the English crown. For many years English rulers had had designs upon the assimilation of Ireland, and one scheme, among many, that was used to accomplish this goal was the granting of land to English and Scotch landlords if they would migrate to Ireland and settle there. Under James I, this policy was pushed vigorously, and many Scots, many of whom were Presbyterians, settled in four northeastern counties of Ireland. One of these counties was Antrim, the home of Alexander Campbell's family. From time to time the English rulers tried to bring the Scotch-Irish under domination of the Anglican church, but there were too many of them with a Presbyterian background for the English scheme to be successful. The strong feelings these people had about a church which was "separate" from the national church of England brought upon them the stigma of "non-conformists," but they referred to themselves simply as "separatists" or "seceders."

Previous to Thomas and Alexander Campbell's coming to America, mass migrations to the new country had taken place. The migrations started in the early 1700's and it is estimated that by 1750 some one hundred thousand of these people had come to American shores. When the Campbells left Ireland, they left Presbyterians they had lived with and understood and, when they arrived in western Pennsylvania, they came to Presbyterian churches made up of people who had carried many of the old ideas of religion and old forms of worship with them. Moving from one country to another, therefore, was not a cultural break. America was a new country in terms of physical resources and economic life; but as Santayana has pointed out, it was a new country with an old mentality; it was "old wine in new bottles." By the time of the American revolution, the Scotch-Irish were to be found in every colony, and it is estimated that in the Pennsylvania region there were some one hundred and thirty settlements. Large numbers were also found in Virginia, Maryland, and what is now Kentucky and Tennessee.

As people moved across the mountains it was more difficult to keep in touch with the parent religious bodies in the old countries, and soon circumstance, along with initiative on the part of some leaders, made for modifications of the old habits of religious life. Even strict bodies, like the Presbyterians, had difficulty keeping their beliefs and practices from being modified as new occasions and new problems arose. For instance, Thomas Campbell faced a problem of sharing the Lord's Supper with Christians who were non-Presbyterians in a community where his church offered the only chance of participating in a religious service. When he extended the invitation to non-Presbyterians to share in the Lord's Supper, he was modifying a strict practice of his own church. This modification of the Lord's Supper, that is, extending a welcome to any Christian of any denomination to the Lord's table, became known as "open communion." Thomas Campbell was reprimanded by the authorities of the Presbyterian church for modifying the practice, and this experience, among other things, was the occasion for his ultimate break with that body. Because of the partly fluctuating and unstable life on the changing frontier and because physical and cultural conditions of the new world sometimes made the duplication of the old worship forms impossible, modifications in many of the inherited practices took shape. Furthermore, the variety of cultural patterns which diverse people from the old countries brought with them soon made America a rich soil for social and religious experimentation. These conditions made it possible for dissenters and enterprising leaders to initiate new congregations and to rob the old ones of their members. Because of a climate of freedom of worship, anyone who could get enough followers to support his cause could walk out of an established group and form his own church.

It was in this open cultural climate of America that Alexander Campbell could initiate a new movement and come to his own personal fulfillment. [2] It was here that he distinguished himself as a preacher and a lecturer; in fact, he made accomplishments in several ways. On one occasion he addressed both Houses of the United States Congress in joint session, and on another he delivered an address before the legislature of the State of Missouri. He served his district as a delegate in re-writing the constitution of Virginia. He gave numerous lectures to colleges, literary and philosophic groups. He took an important part in the great debates of the era, one of the most significant being a debate with Robert Owen, the social experimenter. In the field of religious journalism, in both *The Christian Baptist* and *The Millennial Harbinger,* for over forty years his religious and philosophical ideas helped mold the new country. As the founder, first president, and one of the professors of Bethany College, he achieved stature in the field of education. As founder and leader of the largest Protestant group in the new world, as crusader for a new basis for Christian unity, as philosopher and religious thinker, as debator, journalist, and educator, Alexander Campbell occupies a unique place in its intellectual history. His philosophy and religion has had a dynamic part in the shaping of the American mind.

As frequently occurs in the history of thought, the intellectual phase of the culture of Campbell's time was a course of adjustment of new ways of thinking to old. How could the empirical method, the method which emphasizes the observations which man's sensory organs give him, be used to substantiate traditional doctrines found in the Bible? How could the growing interest in the linguistic and historical methods of scholarship be applied to the Scriptures? How could the new scientific views of the universe and the older views of creation be accommodated? How could the rise of utilitarian ethics with its pleasure-pain principle be incorporated into the Biblical view of morality? How could the rising tide of democracy be brought into a working harmony with ecclesiastical organizations? The answers which Alexander Campbell gave to these and other similar questions make up the central beliefs of his philosophy and religion.

Alexander Campbell is one of those thinkers who realize that experience outgrows the old patterns of thought. He adopts the attitude of seeking to conserve what is of value in the traditional while accepting what seems reasonable in novel developments. To him the relation of older and newer ways of ideas is a course of

---

2 For an excellent account of the historical factors operating at the time of Campbell's life in America, see Arthur Schlesinger, Jr., "The Age of Alexander Campbell," in *The Sage of Bethany,* compiled by Perry E. Gresham (St. Louis: The Bethany Press, 1960) , pp. 25-44.

intellectual accommodation and adaptation. He came to maturity in the early part of the nineteenth century and lived through the middle years of that century as a thinker on the growing edge of religious and philosophical thought. During his life he sought to bring essential religious beliefs and the philosophically novel ideas of his contemporaries into some kind of intellectual harmony.

II

EMPIRICAL METHOD AND THE SCRIPTURES

Whenever Alexander Campbell is driven to basic philosophical principles in his writings, lectures, and debates, he appeals to "the accepted principles of Locke and recent thinkers since him." The "principles" of Locke referred to are the methods of observation, of the careful and cautious scrutiny of sensory experiences and what they yield, the methods which Campbell claims form the basis of science and scholarship. These methods of observation and the careful determination of the facts of experience may be referred to simply as "observational method" or "empirical method." By empirical method is meant that human knowledge originates by means of the sense organs; that out of these sensory impressions are constructed "ideas," and, in turn, these ideas must be brought back to sensory observations for test and verification.

Empirical method as put forth by the thinkers of the age of the Enlightenment, and adopted by Campbell with some modifications, was a reaction to the conceptual methods advocated by some thinkers of their times and of the past. These so-called "rationalists," against whom the empirical revolt took place, had made the conceptual and logical side of experience uppermost. For them sensory experiences must agree with the thought-patterns in the human mind, and if the sensory experiences did not agree with these conceptual forms, then the former must be discarded as false and illusory. Some of the rationalists had gone so far as to advocate the doctrine of "innate ideas," that ideas are somehow imbedded or contained in the human mind even at birth. Against this contention, the empiricists following Locke, adopted two cardinal principles: there are no innate ideas and all simple ideas come from sensation and reflection. With these two principles Campbell is in complete agreement; he says that a child's mind is a "blank tablet" at birth, thus he rejects the theory of innate ideas; he holds that all simple ideas come from sensation and reflection, thus he is empirical in his approach to knowledge.

Although there is considerable similarity in the views held by Campbell and Locke, Campbell is indebted to other thinkers in the empirical movement for many of his ideas. Previous to Locke, there was Francis Bacon, whom Campbell regarded as one of the greatest minds of all time. Bacon's inductive method, the method of starting with minute observations or facts and building up a belief by heaping fact upon fact until a generalization results, was adopted by Campbell in his method of studying the Scriptures. Bacon also made excursions into the study of language, of the relation of words to ideas and to things, and there is some indication that some of Campbell's method of language study stems from Bacon as well as from Locke. The later empiricists, Bishop Berkeley and David Hume, are not among Campbell's heroes; there is little indication that he ever read Berkeley and he rejected Hume as a sceptic. The "recent thinkers" since Locke undoubtedly refers to the Scottish Common-sense realists, Thomas Reid and Dugald Stewart; the latter Campbell called "the greatest of all metaphysicians."

Almost every thinker who followed Locke's empirical approach felt that he had to give an account of the human mind, of the nature of its operations, of its methods of gaining knowledge, and of its scope and limits. Campbell was no exception in this respect, and he made several detailed descriptions of the whole range of sensory experience and the knowledge gained through empirical method. At one place he lists four "powers" of attaining knowledge — instinct, sensation, reason, and faith. [1] He dismisses instinct as being of little or no importance for attaining human knowledge, and then proceeds to give detailed analyses of the nature of sensory experience.

Campbell's description of sensory experience naturally starts with an analysis of the word *sense;* by this he means the "external organs," the "five senses, and that these *five senses* are the only avenues through which intelligence concerning material things can reach us." [2] He goes into much detail on these five senses, starting with smelling, which he thought was the simplest, and then moving to a consideration of tasting, feeling, seeing, and hearing. His analysis follows the usual description of his day on the way these sense organs function and of the sensory experiences they produce in man. The conclusion he draws from these studies is that if a person were destitute of all sensory experiences, he would be nothing but "a lump of insensible matter." This means that a child's mind is a "blank tablet" at birth upon which is inscribed the sense impressions of the external objects he encounters.

Out of these sensory experiences, man constructs the realm of "ideas," that is, using the language of the Enlightenment, ideas are "derived" from sense perceptions. The senses, Campbell says, put us in possession of all the materials upon which the intellect has to work. He compares this process to the manner in which the raw material is first put in the hands of the manufacturer before it can be made to serve the various uses of life. A man's mechanical and intellectual ingenuity is powerless without this sensory material. As

---

[1] *Millennial Harbinger,* 1841, pp. 353-354.
[2] *Campbell-Owen Debate,* I, p. 134.

Campbell put it, "There can be no ship without timber, and no pen knife without metal."

Now, if all ideas are derived from sensory experience, there must be a "model" or "archetype" of each of these ideas which is presented to each sense. This concept of the "archetype" of ideas is not well developed in Campbell's theory; it is obvious, however, that he is following Locke on this point. Take, for instance, Campbell's treatment of the difference between "real" and "imagined" ideas in experience. As objects are presented to the human mind, they are presented with colors, sizes, shapes, and so forth. It is possible for the mind to *abstract* qualities from objects and *compound* them by means of imagination into "ideas" of objects which do not exist. Campbell's example is taken from Locke; the idea of a "centaur" is not real since it is not obtained through the senses.[3] When one begins to check his idea of a centaur against what he has experienced by means of the senses, he cannot find such an object; in other words, there is no archetype of the idea of a centaur found in nature. Thus, ideas constructed in the mind, real or imaginary, must be brought back to sensory experience for their test. Although Campbell never made much of this point, it is clear that he has a correspondence theory of truth, for all ideas must correspond to the reality of the objects that are presented to the senses.

The foregoing theory of sensory experience and the theory of ideas corresponding to archetypes must account for errors both in ideational constructions and in the sensory experiences themselves. The "idea" constructed must come back to sensory experience for its check and test. But what if the senses deceive us, both in the origin of the ideas and in their test? Campbell admits that it is possible for the senses to deceive a person. [4] He acknowledges that either the eyes or the ear, singly and alone, of an individual may deceive that person. He thinks it possible, though less likely, that both senses in conjunction, such as seeing and hearing, might deceive a man. Be this as it may, Campbell places a great trust in the accuracy of sensory experience. He says: "It is indeed contrary to my experience, and I presume contrary to the experiences of millions of my fellow citizens to have been deceived by an object addressed to the eye and the ear at the same time. One may illusively at one time hear a sound, and at another, see a light which has not real existence; but that any person, at one and the same time, ever saw a light and heard a voice unreal, supposes an illusion of two senses, which were I to make my own experience or that of a million of my contemporaries, a rule of faith, I could never believe." [5] In case a man of

3 *Ibid.*, I, p. 143.
4 *Protestant Preacher's Companion*, p. 3.
5 *Ibid.*, p. 3-4.

religion wonders what is so vital in this theory of knowledge and why it is important to Campbell, it can be recalled that in the report of the conversion of Apostle Paul a voice was heard and a light was seen. The authenticity of Paul's experience is established by applying the observational method to the report, that is, by going to the sensory experiences of the people involved at the time the conversion took place. It is difficult for Campbell to believe that a conjunction of hearing and seeing could be erroneous.

While the human mind is described as a "blank tablet," it has some active powers or capacities. The mind perceives, discriminates, compares, abstracts, composes, remembers, and imagines. The perceptions presented to the mind in the life of an individual show how that individual can acquire knowledge of the world directly, that is, how a single individual can observe and construct the ideas which make up his knowledge. It is obvious, however, that one person cannot have sensory knowledge of everything in the world. Sensory experience of every event in the present is impossible because of the very nature of man's limitations in space and time. When it comes to understanding past events, it is impossible for a person to transport himself to a distant time and place and have experiences of people far away from his contemporary scene. Such a condition of human experience means that man must rely upon the "reports" of others, reports of the sensory experiences which they have had.

Campbell shows that a great deal of our knowledge is dependent upon the reports of others from times and places inaccessible to our own observations. Accordingly, the reliability of reports is very important and they must not be accepted uncritically. He proposes a program to be adopted to make our belief in testimonies secure. In a broad and general way, he sets up two criteria at first; 1) does the report seem reasonable to us? 2) does it conform to the criterion for the examination of the testimony of others? The first criterion means that the reasonableness of the report must be something that could have come through the senses, that is, the report must describe things seen and heard, felt and tasted and smelled. The second criterion is much more involved, for it is a means of ascertaining whether one is to believe the reports and have faith in the testimony of others who claim that they experienced such events. This method of test turns into four considerations: 1) In order to judge the *certainty* of facts, of their truth or falsity, we must ask if the facts are what we call "sensible facts," such as "the eyes of the spectators and all their other senses might take cognizance of." 2) We must ask if these facts allegedly sensory in character were "public," that is, open to "attestation" by several or at least more than one person. For instance, note the "public" nature of Jesus' baptism and the numerous persons who saw his ascension.

3) We must examine the facts to see if there are certain "monumental and commemorative" institutions existing from the time of an event to the present which afford a certain kind of historical "attestation" of the facts. 4) Furthermore, we must ascertain if these monumental proofs "existed simultaneously with the transpiration of the facts which they intend to perpetuate." [6]   These criteria, of course, establish baptism and the Lord's Supper as factual events which can be believed on the basis of faith in the reports.

In the process of ascertaining if an event actually took place, Campbell adopts the verification techniques common to an empirical method which is inherent in the English legal system. For instance, one must ask how many people witnessed an event, and the number of witnesses carries great weight on the assumption that it is difficult to mislead a large number of people. One must ask if these witnesses had ample and repeated opportunities for examination of the events they are reporting. Next, it must be asked if the witnesses are reliable, that is, are they cautious, rational, and of a discriminating character. And, if the witnesses first did not believe the fact presented to them but later were convinced and reported what they believed, their testimony is much more valuable, for it apparently moves from scepticism to belief. The case of Thomas' doubt and subsequent belief is a case in point.

Campbell accepts Francis Bacon's definition of a fact as "something said" or "something done." [7] He holds that all true and useful knowledge is acquaintance with facts, that all true science is acquired from the observation and comparison of facts. Furthermore, he adopts Bacon's method of induction, of heaping fact upon fact to secure a generalization, for he thinks that the way to form a clear and definite idea is not by reasoning hypothetically or deductively, but inductively. This method, of course, has been shown to have serious limitations; it surely overlooks the role played by hypothetical reasoning which is so important in modern science, and it neglects deductive means of ascertaining new facts. In the same manner that Bacon went about simply listing all the things which had warmth in them, piling fact on fact about warm things, Campbell goes about piling fact on fact concerning any event he investigated in the Bible. A listing of all the cases of the accounts of baptism can be used to prove that such an event is of significance. This use of induction is Campbell's way of proving that "something said" or "something done" actually took place within the Bible.

Campbell's empirical method carries with it another aspect, an attitude toward speculation, which he apparently took from the

6 *Millennial Harbinger,* 1836, pp. 411-418. Also, see *Campbell-Owen Debate,* I, p. 170.
    7 *Millennial Harbinger,* 1830, p. 9.

Common-sense realist, Dugald Stewart. Stewart summed up his adversity to speculation in these words: "The prejudice, which is commonly entertained against metaphysical speculation seems to arise from two causes: first, from an apprehension, that the subjects, about which they are employed are placed beyond the reach of human faculties; and, second, from a belief that these subjects have no relation to the business of life." [8] Campbell adopts this critical attitude toward speculation upon philosophical matters, for instance, the "essences" and "quintessences" of the Scholastics. He adopts this attitude also toward anything which goes beyond observation in the sciences. But the especial use he makes of it is in application to extra-Biblical matters, to "religious" matters which are found outside the pages of the Bible. In his mind the entire paraphernalia which had grown up outside the Bible, in post-Biblical theologies and creeds, is speculative. What man needs, he thinks, is a fresh approach to the Bible, an approach without pre-conceptions or inherited patterns of interpretation. The inherited patterns of thought contained in much theology, especially in the written creeds of the church, must be cleared away and the mind given a new method of procedure and a new attitude concerning the nature of religious truth. Men must first discover the "facts" of the Bible, and the only way Campbell can conceive of doing this is by a first-hand study of the reports found there, of the words and the sentences, which make up the various books.

This attention to the study of language, to the consideration of the meaning of a word, to the purport of a sentence, to the production of entire documents, is another aspect of Alexander Campbell's scholarly methods. Again, he seems most influenced by Bacon and Locke, and it should be noted that both of these men made significant contributions to language study. Francis Bacon had advocated a careful study of language as providing clues to the nature of objects which the words named. Campbell is in complete agreement with Bacon in holding that the relation between a word and the idea which it represents "is the nearest of all relations in the universe, for the idea is in the word, and the word is in the idea." Bacon claimed that an idea is invisible, inaudible, and unintelligible except in and by a word. In this "symbolic" theory of ideas, it appears that an idea cannot be without an image or a word to represent it. Apparently it is on Bacon's theory of the relation between words and ideas that Campbell builds his view of the Word of God. Since ideas and words are inseparable, the Word of God in the Bible is the Word of God expressed by God, that is, the Word of God in the Bible is the way in which God reveals Himself. God's

8 Dugald Stewart, *The Works of Dugald Stewart,* Seven Vols. (Cambridge: Hilliard and Brown, 1829), I, p. 1.

ideas are so closely related to the language of the Bible that the study of these reports from an empirical standpoint is the only method by which man may now, at this stage in human history, come to know God.

On this theory of language, one might think that the Word of God is completely equated with the words and sentences of the Bible, but this is not entirely clear on Campbell's account. Campbell is not a "literalist" in interpreting the Bible, that is, he did not believe that all figures of speech should be reduced to factual meanings and that the context of each passage should be ignored. He adopts the new scholarly approach to the Bible as literature; he holds that the different books of the Bible are written with specific intents, at specific times, with a specific kind of language. This means that each book should be studied to discover the author's intent in writing it. Special attention should be given to the date of each document. What was the occasion? Is the specific book intended as history, as parable, as allegory, as poetry? To give a literal meaning to a Biblical poem or allegory would be as great a misinterpretation as to mistranslate a vital passage. [9]

With this introductory study of the Bible, the interpretation must then proceed to a study of the words and sentences. This means that the interpreter must go back to the original Hebrew, Greek, or Aramaic and trace each term through its various usages and translations by different authors. Campbell not only believes that this method is the proper way to study the Bible and employs the method himself, but he recommends that all Christian ministers and even laymen adopt this means of Bible study. Carrying out his own program, Campbell made at least two translations or editions of the New Testament. The recommendation of Campbell for this kind of Bible study has a challenging note. Undoubtedly, in his own day there were few, even among his own inner circle, who had the ability, the educational background, or the infinite scholarly patience, to use such a method. And it can be gathered that Campbell recognized this, for somewhere he says that there were only two persons on the North American continent in his day who knew how to read the Bible correctly, and one of these, of course, was himself.

There is another area in the history of religious thought from which Campbell draws his ideas. The development of "covenant" theology had a strong influence on his mind. [10] The division of Biblical history into "stages" is accepted by Campbell, and he uses these divisions in order to answer many puzzling questions about

---

9 *The Christian System,* pp. 3-5.
10 *Campbell-Owen Debate, II,* pp. 97-124. Campbell gives several accounts of the covenants, but this reference contains the most complete one.

the origin of certain religious and cultural elements in universal human history. These stages of religious development which he thinks are contained in the Bible are put on a vertical scale, the latest being the most important. The first and "primitive" stage of man was that of Edenic purity. This was the state of man's condition in the Garden of Eden, a state in which there was no special need for revelation, for man could perceive God directly. Man walked in the cool of the evening with God; he talked and even ate with Him. With the advent of the Fall, man lost his intimate fellowship with God, and God retired from the presence of man and the world. In the Fall, man lost more elaborate spheres in which the sensory organs could act. Thus, man's noetic faculties were limited, and henceforth, "revelation" was necessary as the only method by which God and man could have communication.

The patriarchal age, from Adam to Moses, was an age wherein successive revelations and covenants were made. The institutions of religion sought to deal with the human race in its infancy. Man did not develop these institutions, but God revealed them gradually. In this age, religion involved sacrifices, keeping the Sabbath, and priesthood. The Jewish dispensation was the period from Moses to the time of the Christian dispensation. It was the era of national religion. The covenant of this period was the Decalogue, the laws of which had to be kept rigorously because the Decalogue preserved in written form the knowledge of God. The Christian dispensation was still another advance in human development through Biblical times. The laws of the kingdom in the new dispensation were delivered at Pentecost. The rules and regulations of the church, then, are found after the event of Pentecost, and not before it.

The implications of this approach to Biblical history are many, but in passing it should be noted that the theory of "dispensations" and of gradual revelations within the Bible led Campbell and his followers to place the New Testament above the Old Testament in importance and to coin the phrase: "Old Testament for the Jews; New Testament for the Christians." Furthermore, by making the Christian dispensation begin with Pentecost, Campbell makes the *Book of Acts of Apostles* assume a place of supreme importance, even above the *Gospels*. One very far reaching result of this theory is to place the teachings of Jesus in the era preceding the Christian stage; this distinction makes the faith and practice of the Christian church more Pauline than Christological.

Campbell thinks that revealed religion is confined to the Bible, and when his empirical method of study along with his adverse attitude toward "speculation" is brought to bear on religious matters, several implications follow. Any belief purporting to be religious is "speculative" unless it can be empirically ascertained from the pages of the Bible. [11] The Bible alone must be taken as the guide for faith and practice, and any creed or belief formulated in such a way that it does not mirror an idea in the Bible is regarded as "speculative." This does not mean, however, that statements of belief are not worth constructing, but they must be tested by the accounts in the Bible, and they must be re-written from time to time as better scholarship shows what the Bible really means. But the creeds and statements of belief which have grown up since Bible days are not "revelations"; they are man-made things, and as such, have become the source of dissension and of division within Christendom. [12] Sometimes Campbell carries this view so far as to claim that religious language not recorded in the Bible should be discarded; in this respect, he leaves little if no room in his theory for the ideas, vocabularies, and institutions of men which have expanded beyond the limitations of the experience of the people of Biblical times.

Campbell's approach to the Scriptures involves four important assumptions about them and how they are to be studied. In the first place, the Bible must be accepted as the Word of God with different levels of religious development contained within it. Second, the Bible must be studied by moving outside each book to determine its authorship and its authenticity, and by moving inside each book to understand the kind of language used and the literal or figurative meanings employed. Third, the Bible is a "book of facts" and must be studied with an empirical method which first observes what is there and then proceeds to look at the sensory experiences of the people who reported the events and to pile fact upon fact to make secure a belief about any specific event. Fourth, the establishment of any belief or practice must be ascertained by determining if it has a Scriptural basis and how certain it is.

The authenticity of specific practices in the Christian life are to be determined by noting all the instances in which such practices occurred in the Bible. Baptism, as one of the most universal practices of Christians, can be proved to be a rightful practice by consulting all those cases in which it is mentioned in the Bible. [13] The question of who should perform the baptismal act is settled by Scriptural references. On this basis, Campbell thinks any baptized believer proper to administer the rite of baptism to another. The manner in which the baptismal act is performed is determined by a linguistic analysis of the word, and Campbell thinks that the original meaning of the word is "immerse."

---

[11] *Campbell-Owen Debate,* I, p. 221.
[12] *The Christian System,* pp. 126-128.
[13] See the *Campbell-Walker Debate,* especially p. 138; the entire volume is devoted to the issue of baptism.

The practice of observing the "Lord's Supper" is determined by the same empirical approach to the Scriptures. In the first place, Campbell tries to establish the fact that the observance of the Lord's Supper has nothing to do with the older stages of religious development recorded in the Bible. It is not a continuation of Passover; it is a new and completely different event; it is a "Christian" event. Through his careful examination of the different events of observing the Lord's Supper recorded in the Scriptures, Campbell comes to the conclusion that the Lord's Supper is a celebration of the resurrection of Christ. In the Christian dispensation, the Lord's Day is considered to be the first day of the week and not the seventh; thus the keeping of the Sabbath is a Jewish custom and not Christian. Since there is no record of any one specific manner in which the early Christians administered the Lord's Supper, Campbell thinks that this should be left to the discretion and good taste of the communicants. [14]

One of the most troublesome problems for all reformers who wanted to purify the practices of Christianity from the early Puritans to the Restoration leaders is that of the form and organization of the church. Campbell tries to make the Bible the chief authority on this matter, of course, but the problem is complicated by the variety of reports within the Scriptures and by the widened experience with social organization developed in post-Biblical history. Campbell does not want the term "government" applied to church organizations; [15] but it is not an easy matter to find a specific form of organization within the New Testament which can be adopted as the rightful one, for there are many forms of church organization found there. Nevertheless, there seems to be a point which Campbell can be certain of in his findings — the local church is the principal "unit" in power and authority. [16] This position concerning the sovereignty of the local unit can be explained by two facts of human experience, of which one Campbell seems unaware and the other he assumes in his general philosophy but never makes explicit. The first fact concerns the conditions under which institutions sometimes develop when there is no central and coordinating agency. They grow up, each independent of the other, and their only connections with similar units are acquaintances with some strong leaders like Paul or Peter or James; sometimes their similarities are due to a common founder, or to exchange of letters, or to reports from travelling brothers. The assumed, but unexplicit philosophy, which is undoubtedly found in Campbell is his adherence to nominalism, the view that only "particular units" are real and

---

14 *The Christian Baptist,* VII, p. 655.
15 *Millennial Harbinger,* 1858, p. 449.
16 *Ibid.,* 1850, p. 286.

that all systems relating such units are abstractions or generalizations built up from such units. Proof of this point comes from Campbell's view of "systems" of nature as described in *The Christian System*. It is significant to point out here that his nominalistic philosophy, starting with individual units as real, does not mean that units cannot be related in system. In fact, each unit gets part of its meaning in existence by its cooperation in a system. Thus, the local unit or church is never wholly autonomous or independent of all other churches in a Christian system of units. [17]

The power and authority of the local church gives it the right to set apart certain individuals as ministers and to "call" a minister of its own choosing. When the matter of cooperative work among the churches became a problem, Campbell gradually changed his more radical beliefs about organizations attached to the church proper. At first, he wanted all organizations outside the church proper rooted out of existence, for they are non-Biblical. [18] This meant that such organizations as missionary societies, Bible schools, even colleges and seminaries, along with higher boards of cooperation are non-Biblical and should be iconoclastically destroyed. But time, circumstance, common sense, and expanding human problems gradually changed Campbell's mind on these matters.

The successes and failures of the application of Campbell's methods to the ascertainment of Christian faith and practice cannot be overlooked. The attempt to "restore" Christianity to a simplicity of faith, like the simplicity of the Confession, and to the simplicity of practices, like Baptism and the Lord's Supper, has its merits, for it makes commitment to Christ primary and it makes meaningful His commemoration. On the other hand, Campbell's approach to the Scriptures brought sorrows of further divisions among his followers. The reforms or purifications of the practices of the churches became the occasions of debates and conflicts among Campbell's followers. [19] Not the least among these conflicts has been the use of artistic and aesthetic forms and meanings, like the

[17] *Millennial Harbinger*, 1858, p. 450. "All churches being equally independent, they must be severally consulted in all appointments of a general import and significance, equally depending upon them for countenance and aid."

[18] Campbell's early position of missionary societies, for instance, is stated in *The Christian Baptist*, I, p. 15. There he claims that missionary societies are "unauthorized" and a "hopeless" means of converting the world. By 1832, in *The Millennial Harbinger*, he had changed his mind, as he writes: "... and I have no hesitation in saying, that if all was done at home which our means could effect, we would unite with the whole church of God in any evangelical mission to lands and tribes where the name of the Lord has not been named." p. 616. See also, *Millennial Harbinger*, 1833, pp. 469-470.

[19] For a detailed study of this problem, see A. T. DeGroot, *The Grounds of Divisions Among the Disciples of Christ*, Chicago: privately printed, 1940.

use of music, of pianos and organs, or any instrument which makes the aesthetic part of religious experience of importance.

Some other implications about Campbell's method and his view of revealed religion as confined to the Scriptures should be pointed out. Like others of his age who shared an interest in the functions of language, he tries to offer some explanation of its origin. It will be recalled that Campbell begins his analysis of the human mind by maintaining that it is a "blank tablet" at birth. Furthermore, he limits the "inventive" powers of the human mind in a way which seals off the possibility of man inventing a language on his own. Campbell adopts the current psychology of his day which maintained that a child must first hear someone speak, and the child would never learn a language unless he imitated others around him who taught him the sounds to make and how to attach certain references to those sounds. But if one pushes the inquiry back in history, the question arises of how the first man learned to speak. Campbell sees only three possible explanations of this phenomenon; that man taught himself to speak, that God inspired man with the wisdom to invent a language; that God Himself spoke to man, thus giving him language through the direct imitation of God's voice. Of course, Campbell never intimates what particular dialect God used when first speaking to man nor does he attempt to give a rational explanation of how the diversity of languages developed. He is aware of the common roots of certain words, a discovery which language scholars of his times had made. But all he asserts is that all languages have a common source and this common source he holds to have originated at some place in Biblical history.

Another problem for Campbell's theory is the necessity of explaining how the different non-Christian religions developed. What is the origin of "Mohammetism," as he called it? In agreement with his assumption of early man's common geographic home and a common origin of language, Campbell believes that all the spiritual ideas of non-Christian religions are borrowed from the Bible. [20] The origin of spiritual ideas found in other religions is accounted for by his theory of the covenants. During the age of "national" religion, the various peoples began to migrate over the earth taking with them the spiritual ideas revealed to them by God. Thus, he holds that there is not a spiritual idea in the world which is not borrowed from the Bible.

There are limitations set upon Campbell's thought by the times in which he lived and by the assumptions he made about philosophy and religion. He was in the forefront of the empiricist

[20] *Campbell-Owen Debate*, II, pp. 97-124.

movement as it took shape in his day, it is true, but even sensory experiences which he deems so important in establishing scientific, philosophical, and religious beliefs, have been deepened and widened in subsequent analysis. Empiricism came to be much wider in scope than the limitations to the five senses he sets upon it, and it has become much deeper in its analysis of human feelings, desires, emotions, and relations. Conclusions Campbell draws about the origin of language and the occurrence of spiritual ideas in non-Christian religions, valiant as they are as an attempt at consistency for his empirical method and its relation to revealed religion, would hardly pass as adequate explanations today. His method of heaping fact upon fact to prove that something in the Bible really happened has its merits and its limitations. It is true that his method makes men pay attention to what is actually recorded in the Scriptures, and it cautions us not to read into the reports inferences which are not there, and this is significant for scholarship. But subsequent thought has shown that it is not enough to state that a fact occurs or exists. Events are not self-explanatory; it is more important to probe into the deeper meanings, the richer meanings of any event, and this is true for events like Baptism and the Lord's Supper.

Alexander Campbell's attempt to bring scholarly methods to the Bible is admirable, and it is a legacy which time and patient study have vindicated. His recommendations that all ministers become masters of such methods of study, entail, perhaps, more than he envisioned. Along with a knowledge of Hebrew, Greek, and Aramaic, it is necessary to be a master of the techniques of scrutinizing the earliest documents which establish the authoritative texts of the Bible. This area alone is a lifetime of work and commitment. Historical contexts, which he desired so zealously to use, are not always easy to determine. Philological studies of the origins, of the usages, and of the methods of comparison and contrast applied to symbols, are arduous tasks. Archeological inquiries which dig deep into the past, find new artifacts and symbolic remains, must be interpreted. The understanding of the documents and of the contexts of Biblical history is an increasingly complicated and difficult task. Campbell's belief that the common man can read the text of the Bible and obtain a reasonably clear understanding of it is an indication of his tremendous faith in every man's ability. The approach to the Scriptures which he advocates is now specialized with the linguist, historian, philologist, and archeologist all contributing to modern man's understanding. The minister and the layman are now dependent upon specialists for the substance of their beliefs. Even a sampling of the scholarship necessary for an intelligent understanding of the Scriptures today shows how one cannot become dogmatic about any specific point. The uninformed may become dogmatic, but this dogmatism can be exposed, and scholarly humility now becomes the proper attitude.

And yet, it is difficult to see how any person inside the Christian movement, or even any objective scholar outside of it, can deny the deep and penetrating insights about life recorded in the Bible. These reports are of more than literary value, although they contain some of the highest achievements in written expression. The experiences reported there are those of sensitive and critical men as they grappled with the challenging problems of human existence, aspiration, faith, and personal and associated living. And it is difficult to see how any intelligent person can approach these reports without the tools of scholarship, which he would use in the understanding of any other document of far-reaching historical and life significance. The Scriptures are to be constantly examined and re-examined in the light of new thought and new techniques of study. The record there is like the record left in an autobiography — it is an expression of life — a response — and the meaning of it contains material which is a perennial source for wonderment and study. Campbell's approach to the Biblical documents is wise and fruitful, and it forms a link in an ever-deepening understanding of its truths. These truths are not based upon the methods of authority and tradition, methods which Campbell rejected and even scorned; they are truths ascertained by vigorous minds not afraid to search and to find.

III

REVELATION, REASON, AND FAITH

Alexander Campbell's religious philosophy emphasizes the primacy of observational methods and their application to the Bible as the revealed Word of God. But like all empiricists, he holds that observational theories and methods are matters of emphasis, not exclusive of all other aspects of the knowing experience. Thus, Campbell gives some account of the role of reason, as well as of sense perception; at the same time, these two elements of philosophical method are brought into harmony with the traditional religious methods of revelation and faith.

Campbell accepts a belief in revelation, but it is a revelation with limitations and modifications of the traditional theme; his view of revelation is tempered by reason. Furthermore, he regards the Bible as the revealed Word of God, but differences appear between the view he holds and that of some other religious thinkers, for he holds that while the Bible is the source of all revelations, these revelations are not of equal stature and worth. Some revelations belong to the childhood of the human race and are to be regarded and treated as such. These earlier covenants cannot be made the basis for faith and practice in the present. The successive revelations finally evolved into the Christian dispensation or era, the last and most important for contemporary man, and according to Campbell's view, this new dispensation began at Pentecost. Thus, while claiming an orthodox position for himself by appeal to the revealed Word, he could attack other self-styled orthodox positions by use of his critical approach to stages of religious evolution. From this vantage point, Campbell attacked the Baptists, Presbyterians, and Catholics. [1] On the other hand, Campbell shares many of the doctrines of traditionalists on other matters because these are supported by Biblical facts; among these beliefs are those in miracles, angels, heaven, hell, and other familiar themes.

The most fundamental belief which challenges religious and philosophical inquiry and which points up the relations of revelation, reason, and faith concerns the origin in man's experience of the idea of God. That man has the idea of God in his consciousness

---

[1] Campbell had three debates with Presbyterian ministers. In 1820 he debated John Walker, a Seceder Presbyterian; in 1823 he debated W. L. Maccalla; and in 1843 he debated N. L. Rice. Henry Clay was the moderator for the Rice debate. In 1837 Campbell had a debate with Archbishop Purcell, a Catholic.

is not doubted. But the question is: how and by what methods did the idea of God enter the human mind? Campbell sees this problem in its full force and meaning. He writes: "But the difficulty is — how did the idea originate? By what process could it have been engendered? Where was the archetype in nature to suggest (consistently with the analysis of the human mind) the remotest idea of a Creator, or any other idea concerning spiritual things?" [2] That man has within his consciousness and experience "the existence of this Creative power," Campbell recognizes. Furthermore, it is not the Christian religion alone which possesses the idea of God. In his survey of comparative religions, he found that all nations had originally "some idea of the existence of a Great First Cause." [3]

Campbell surveys the various possibilities of the origin of the idea of God. In the course of his inquiry, he considers sense perception, imagination, invention, and reason as sources of the idea of God. Since he holds that all ideas in the human mind come from a sense perception of objects external to us and from an internal sense of happenings inside our bodies and minds, then it would appear that he must hold that the idea of God must enter the mind through man's sensory experience; that is, either by some observation of fact outside of us or by some internal awareness of the existence of God must be the source of our idea of Him. The notion that the idea of God comes through an internal awareness of God is discarded because Campbell thinks that we are not born with any "innate" ideas. The view that we actually perceive God outside of us is rejected also because we cannot find any "archetype" or model in nature of the idea of God.

If man cannot find the idea of God in his sensory experiences and cannot find any model of the idea of God in nature to which his idea may conform, then is it not possible that the idea of God is fashioned in the imagination of man? To this contention Campbell has some pointed things to say when the argument for the "imaginative" origin of the idea of God is first introduced by Robert Owen in their famous debate. Campbell replied to Owen: "I am just now told by Mr. Owen, that the idea of God obtained this universality through imagination. Now let us try the merits of this solution. Imagination, all writers agree, has not the power of creating any new idea. It has the power of analyzing, combining, compounding, and new-modifying all the different ideas presented to it: but imagination has no creative power." [4] In order to drive home his point, Campbell appeals to concurrence with Locke and

2 *Campbell-Owen Debate*, I, p. 49.
3 *Ibid.*, p. 49.
4 *Campbell-Owen Debate*, I, p. 116.

Hume, as these men he thought had the most respectable philosophies in the Christian and "infidel" schools.

According to Campbell, the human intellect has no creative power. This view has a special philosophical meaning, and its complexities must be understood so that we can know what the human intellect can and what it cannot do. Apprehension of Campbell's rejection of the imaginative origin of the idea of God rests upon this important point. If one conceives experience as composed of "matter" and "form," in the classical sense in which Campbell does, then the limitations of reason can be pointed up. For instance, in the material world, the human intellect is powerless to create one particle of matter. Man can change material objects from one medium to another, like making wood into furniture, but man cannot create nor can he destroy one single piece of original matter. On the notion of "forms," it is the imaginative function of the mind to bring forth forms of things unknown, and while imagination can range widely, imagination is powerless to bring forth "new forms," for what forms it produces are always analogous to the forms of things already known. It is true that the imagination has the power to turn "forms" into specific "shapes," but the latter are mere abstractions and combinations of the former, which are uncreated by man and impossible to destroy. To maintain that man can form the idea of God is to make the idea of God a "fiction" of the imagination; furthermore, this denies God has any reality outside of human minds.

If the human intellect has no power of creativity in producing new particles of matter or of destroying them and if it has no power of creativity in constructing new forms or of destroying them, what, then, is its role in human experience? What can reason do when it is limited by restrictions in the realm of matter and form? The answer to this question, as Campbell gives it, goes back to the starting place of all human knowing, to the initial proposition of his empirical method in which he maintains that all simple ideas come from sensation and reflection. The human mind has the power to discriminate, to mark off one name, one thing, or one attribute of a thing from another. It can compare and abstract from sensory experience presented to it; it can formulate conceptions about this sensory world; it can formulate propositions about sensations and can make deductions from them. Since for Campbell all knowledge originates in the senses, and reason cannot create these sensations, it is the power of reason or the intellect to "work upon" this material which the senses present to the mind. [5] Thus, reason has its powers and its limitations; it is not completely restricted nor is it completely omnipotent.

5 *Ibid.,* I, pp. 142-143.

Campbell thinks that the Deists placed too much emphasis upon the power of reason and had not recognized its limitations, but the criticism he makes of the Deists is not on the grounds described above. For the Deists also held that man cannot create a particle of matter; also, the Deists did not hold that man could create natural forms. They did hold, however, that the invention of new forms out of the ones given in experience gave man a kind of creativity. The crux of the issue between Campbell and the Deists on this point is that he does not think that the Deists could account for some institutions of human culture purely on the imaginative creativity of man; what is needed is a belief in Biblical revelation to account for many of these. The notion of God, for instance, Campbell thinks had to come from Biblical revelation. Campbell's criticism of the Deists stems from the latter's denial of the need for Biblical revelation as a source of many of man's ideas and institutions found in human culture.

Campbell regards himself an expert on the movement of Deism, and there are many indications that he read with great care many of the writings of this group. [6] The most significant criticism which he makes of the Deists on the role of reason appears in one passage where he wrote: "Some philosophers have almost deified reason, and given to it a creative and originating power. They eulogized the light of reason and the light of nature, that one would imagine reason to be the *sun*; rather than an eye; a revelation, rather than the power of apprehending and enjoying it." [7] In this statement we obtain both his negative response to the Deists and his positive response to what he thought is the proper role of reason in regard to revelation. He attributed to the Deists the view that reason is revelation itself, and this may be taken to mean that the "reason" in men's minds applied to natural events is sufficient for man's understanding of them and of the God responsible for them. Both Campbell and the Deists used Locke as their point of departure in determining the role that reason plays in ascertaining knowledge, but Campbell combines the account given in the *Essay Concerning Human Understanding* with Locke's other work of *The Reasonableness of Christianity*, while the Deists ignored many parts of the latter work.

Campbell's answer to the question of the origin of the idea of God is that the idea originates in Biblical revelation; yet, at the same time he speaks of how "all nature vouches the existence of God." At one point in trying to draw Robert Owen out in their

---

6 For an excellent study of Campbell's reaction to Deism, see Robert Frederick West, *Alexander Campbell and Natural Religion* (New Haven: Yale University Press, 1948).

7 *Popular Lectures and Addresses*, p. 117.

debate, Campbell makes clear his position on revelation as the source of the idea of God. He says: "I boldly assert here, and I court objection to the assertion, that every particle of sound reasoning, and all facts and documents in the annals of time, compel us to the conclusion that the idea and name of God first entered the human family by revelation. No man ever uttered a sentence more unphilosophic, more contrary to human experience, observation, and right reason, than Mirabeau, when he declared that *savages* invented the idea and name of God and spiritual existences." [8] Thus, Campbell holds that revelation is the source of the idea of God; that the idea neither originated in men's sense-perception nor in his natural observations nor was the idea invented by men's imagination. However, in other places and in different contexts, Campbell gives *arguments* for the existence of God which belong to the philosophical tradition that takes reason as the point of departure. In this respect, Campbell is like other religious thinkers who rely upon arguments to prove the existence of God without recourse to revelation.

For instance, when Campbell adopts the argument from cosmology, he does so with a sophistication not usually found in ordinary theological circles. On the view he developed, God did not create the universe because He had the wisdom to design it; nor did He create the universe because he had the power to create it. Wisdom is a passive instrument, and Campbell joins those thinkers who have held that ideas do not have the power to create their own images in this world, a position of historical importance ever since Aristotle's criticism of Plato's doctrine of ideas. This notion was revived by Thomas Aquinas and the criticism of Plato is stated again with more force. How can a bare, abstract idea be invested with the power to create its own image in the world as we know it? Even later when the realm of ideas became associated with the intellect of God, as in Leibniz, the argument still states that even God's intellect or wisdom could not by itself create the world. The outcome of this train of thought was that other parts of God's nature had to create the world, rather than His intellect. Campbell follows this line of thought.

The other line of argument adopted by Campbell is that God did not create the world "because He had the power to create it.'" This position may seem paradoxical, for it would seem that "power" by definition is some kind of active force, and not a passive instrument as Campbell defines it. Campbell did not analyze this point in detail, but the gaps can be filled in by reference to the history of the idea.. For those who have tried to make the cosmological

8 *Campbell-Owen Debate,* I, p. 154.

argument depend upon force and movement were caught in the difficulties of showing how God is an "unmoved mover"; and as an unmoved mover, naturally He is passive, even though He is the source of movement and force. As an unmoved mover, yet the source of all movement and force, God's power was defined as passive.

What Campbell does with these two alternatives, God's wisdom and God's power, as explanations for the creation of the universe is to reject them; he holds that it is another part of God's nature which is the active instrument through which the universe came to be. For Campbell, "Goodness alone is necessarily, eternally, and immutable active." [9] God's will is intelligent, that is, His will is somehow related to the logical consistency of His intellect, and somehow God's will is guided by the wisdom of His intellect. But the main point is that God's will *radiates,* and therefore this is the sense in which He is the First Cause; and God's will *attracts* and this is the sense in which He is the Final Cause.

The use of the argument of Final Cause is also an attempt to appeal to the rationality of man, either in preference to the appeals of revelation or as a supplement to them. Sometimes this argument is called the "teleological argument," or the argument from the belief that there are purposes or goals running through man's experience and the universe as a whole. On Campbell's view, God as Final Cause is the source of "attraction" or a kind of pull which God has upon the world which He created. God is attracting all of the various parts of nature to Himself, and there is thus a kind of destiny to be fulfilled by everything in creation. Sometimes the argument takes the form of holding that there is a "design" to all creation, an order and regularity to all parts of nature for which God alone is responsible. Campbell holds that the whole universe, both in its general laws and in its particular arrangements, is "one immense system of means and ends, suggesting to the true philosopher one great First Cause and one grand Last End, between which all things exist."

The manner in which Campbell united the notions of revelation and reason in determining the existence of God, and thereby setting himself off from the philosophic position entertained by the Deists, is succinctly put in his own words: "In order to establish the true line of demarcation in this matter, I affirm, first that there is a God, all nature cries aloud through her works. But we must have ears to hear this voice. In other words, all things around us and within us prove the existence of God when that idea is originated." [10]

9 *Popular Lectures and Addresses,* p. 164.
10 *Campbell-Owen Debate,* I, p. 133.

In this passage it is clear that Campbell means that the idea of God originates in revelation; but once man has the idea of God, then he can employ rationalistic arguments to prove His existence. In another context, Campbell asserts the role of revelation, but goes directly to a statement of rationalistic proofs. He says, "It is from his word and his works we learn the being and perfections of God." [11] Then, he proceeds to quote the most famous Scripture which supports the teleological argument: "the heavens declare His glory, and the firmament showeth his handy works." He goes on to say that "creation reveals the knowledge, the wisdom, and the goodness of God."

The cosmological and teleological proofs for the existence of God are blended together in one of Campbell's most poetic passages. He says: "There is a reason for every thing, if there be any reason for any thing. Of what use light, if there be not an eye? And what use an eye, if there be not light? Creator and creature are correlates. The one implies the other. There is, therefore, in the human mind, a necessity for the being and perfections of God. His existence is essential to ours; but our existence is not essential to his. We *are*, because he *was*. Had he not been, we never could have been. We are not self-existent. He must, then, be self-existent; consequently, infinite, eternal, and immutable." [12] Campbell's arguments for the existence of God proceed, as we have seen, from two sources: one is from revelation or the Word of God; the other is from reason or inference from the "works of God." Here is an unusual blending of revealed and natural religion. On the one hand, Campbell attacks the Deists who tried to argue for the existence of God on the basis of reason alone; at the same time, he supplements Biblical views of revelation with post-Biblical arguments based upon reason. [13]

To the questions of why revelation is needed and what is learned through revelation, Campbell thinks that no "natural religion" could give answers. On this point he broke with Locke, at least in part. Revelation is needed, Campbell thinks, in order for man to learn about the institutions of society. [14] He holds that the rational powers of man could not have constructed these institutions; they could only be known by God's revelation of them to man at various times in Biblical history. After the fulfillment of time, of course, God revealed the institution of the church, hence this institution was not a human construction, not constructed out of man's natural rational powers or his imaginative powers. This

11 *The Christian System,* p. 20.
12 *Popular Lectures and Addresses,* p. 163.
13 *Campbell-Owen Debate,* I, p. 133.
14 *Ibid.,* I, p. 133.

is plainly at odds with the Deists who attacked many of the established institutions such as the family, law, governments, and economic systems as humanly devised organizations. Of course, among the Deists' list of humanly devised institutions was placed the church.

The roles of revelation and reason in human experience have been related traditionally to some view of the nature of faith. Campbell's account of the nature of faith appears to take two forms: 1) faith is *acceptance* of certain statements or propositions about what is seen, heard, felt, or otherwise experienced by other persons; and this account includes the acceptance of a certain statement as a fact; 2) faith is a kind of *trust* in the source of belief, that is, in the person who relates the experience. It is here that Campbell's empirical method as he conceives it plays a significant part. Our experience is such that we are dependent upon others from childhood for certain knowledge about experience. Campbell says that we take "our first step in the intellectual, moral, and physical worlds by faith." This kind of faith is a "trust," and Campbell describes it thus: "Must it (an infant) experiment with poison or with the asp, the adder, the basilisk, the fire, the flood, the innumerable physical dangers around it, or implicitly believe its nurse, and walk by faith in her traditions." [15] This kind of faith is a trust or commitment to a person.

But Campbell thinks that there is another meaning of faith, a meaning which stems from another aspect of his theory of knowledge. While the integrity and reliability of the reporter must be determined for this sheds light upon the accuracy of the facts reported, the important part of the method of establishing a belief must be the determination of the fact itself. Faith here involves acceptance of a statement as a fact; it is faith in a proposition or factual statement. The facts reported must be "sensible facts," such as "the eyes of the spectators and all their other senses might take cognizance of." These facts must have an open and public character about them so that they can be scrutinized in the severest way. Thus, esoteric facts or subjective experiences so private as to elude this open and public character and to be incapable of the closest investigation by others are ruled out. Furthermore, our belief is aided if there is some continuity from the first occurrence of factual events down through history to the present, such as may be found in certain "commemorations" which have been "institutionalized." The power of belief is strengthened if the commemorations developed at the time of the first occurrence of the fact, and not subsequently. The implication of this statement is that events and commemorations of such events are much more authentic if

15 *Popular Lectures and Addresses*, p. 119.

they can be found in the Bible; they are less authentic, and thus non-essential, if found in post-Biblical history. Any belief or practice that could not be traced to the report of it in Biblical times is discarded, or at least held to be a man-made thing. All of the items of faith are ascertained by the application of observational method to the Scriptures. And Campbell thinks that the kind of faith generated by his empirical method is so certain and secure that if anyone doubted his procedure, he would be striking at the very heart of both science and religion.

Campbell's account of faith allowed him to emphasize two important meanings of it; one is the trust one is to have in Christ and the other is the mental acceptance of statements of fact about Christ which cannot be doubted. Campbell seeks to make man's ultimate commitment hang upon the acceptance of a factual statement. He says, "Peter had the honor of making the first clear, explicit, and correct confession of *the faith,* ever made upon earth. When all the apostles were interrogated by the Lord in his own person concerning their views of himself, Peter thus spoke, 'We believe and are sure that THOU ART THE MESSIAH, THE SON OF THE LIVING GOD'." [16] The "fact" of Jesus' Messiahship is a "supernatural fact," but it is understood through reason, and it is taken on faith — both a faith which means a trust in Christ and a faith which means mental acceptance of the statement concerning His Messiahship. It is the public acceptance of this statement, that is, before witnesses as testifiers of something said or something done by the believer that Campbell makes the basic requirement of being a Christian. The mental assent to this statement becomes the simplest intellectual entrance into the Kingdom, an intellectual assent which is devoid of the long and obscure statements found in the historic creeds of the traditional churches.

While trust in Christ and a faith in the proposition that He is the Messiah offered a simple formula for becoming a disciple, and it is to be admired for its simplicity, the full context of Campbell's views on faith comes at the end of a study of the "facts." We study and learn and know in order to believe. We learn and know before we believe; we do not believe in order to know. The acceptance of any statement about Jesus as the Christ is founded upon a careful study of the Bible. But this is not all; reason is applied to what is read. The reader must first ask if the statements read are reasonable to himself. He must determine whether or not the testimony of others is reliable. After the application of this observational method to the Scriptures, then the reader arrives at his beliefs. As Campbell has no place for "personal" or "subjective"

16 *Campbell-Owen Debate,* II, p. 140.

revelation in post-Biblical times, the only basis for the formation of belief was what man reads and finds reasonable in the Bible. Revelation in Biblical times has revealed new facts to men's minds. In Campbell's words: "The term revelation, in its strict acceptation amongst intelligent Christians, means nothing more nor less than a Divine communication concerning spiritual and eternal things, a knowledge of which man could never have attained by the exercise of his reason upon material and sensible objects." [17]   Thus, supernatural facts entered human experience, but it was left for some men to report these facts, to give testimony concerning them. Thus, one meaning of faith for Campbell is put in this context: "Faith is the simple belief of testimony, or confidence in the word of another." [18]   In matter of priority, revelation had to come first, for the "fact" precedes the report of it, and the report or testimony precedes a faith of the report.

Campbell maintains that commemorative institutions, such as Baptism and the Lord's Supper, have more power for belief in them if their origins can be traced to Biblical times and then shown to have existed from Biblical times in historical continuities down to the present. This position, however, involves him in one of the most difficult philosophical problems of all time, namely, the problem of cause and effect relationships.

Campbell is aware of some of the difficulties in disentangling cause and effect relationships, especially those involving historical continuities. As far as can be discerned, he never gave the problem of cause and effect itself a technical treatment, and he seems oblivious to the devastating criticism which Hume made of the traditional view of the causal relation. Campbell simply took for granted that there can be no event without a cause in the physical and cultural worlds; in this respect, he appears to have followed Locke and the Scottish common-sense realists in his adoption of the principles of causality.

What intrigues Campbell about the relation of cause and effect was not the philosophical problem of the occurrence and interpretation of the relation, but how this relation can occur in the human world, especially in human history. [19]   Adopting the assumption that every event must have a cause, which is the principal means by which rational explanations are made of any and all events, he applies this principle to the problem of trying to explain the peculiar behavior of the people in Bible times when an overwhelming change entered their behavior. How could one explain

[17] *Campbell-Owen Debate,* I, pp. 141-142.
[18] *Millennial Harbinger,* 1836, p. 166.
[19] *Popular Lectures and Addresses,* p. 49.

the extraordinary actions of the men depicted in the Bible? The reports found in the Bible show that the characters often did not believe what they had seen or heard or otherwise experienced. Yet, these Biblical characters were confronted with some "indubitable" facts. Later they changed their whole mode of living and reconstructed their lives. [20] How can this behavior be explained? Campbell thinks it absurd to claim that their mode of living changed without an adequate cause. It is with this kind of causal explanation that he tries to make a case for "revealed" religion, that God is the initiating cause in the change which took place in these Biblical men and women. Campbell can think of no other way to explain these great and momentous changes in human life.

Campbell recognizes that the disentanglement of the causal forces operating in human history is a difficult task to perform. The chain of causes is long and intertwined. He understands that the state of society in his day in the United States and England, in Europe and the world, was the effect of a thousand causes, some of these causal lines cooperating, others antagonistic to the main trend. The history of all these competing and cooperating causes he thinks is impossible to trace out in its fullness. He assumes, however, that the causes were operating even though men were not aware of them. The various causes may first be hidden in the "deep and unexplored recesses of human nature"; they may work for a time "like a secret fire under the mountains" where they are unnoticed and unobserved. But on the occasion of some crisis these causal forces may produce an earthquake or a revolution. Then, of course, the causal forces come to light and they are observed by man because they have impressed themselves upon him. All these causes, now hidden, now apparent, have come to fruition in the present, and Campbell thinks that his own age must be understood in this manner. This is the case, he thinks, with regard to the relation of the fall of the Roman empire to his own day. He holds that there is a connection between the fall of Rome and the society in which he lived, but he hesitates to trace out the original foundations of the series of revolutions which broke that empire into its various parts. There are too many inaccessible facts to make a clear case for specific causal connections between the past and the present.

The belief that every event must have a cause is part of the rationality which makes up the "reasonableness" of the age of the Enlightenment. Campbell accepts this method of reasonableness, and he carries it so far that even the miracles must be explained,

---

[20] See also, *Protestant Preachers' Companion*, p. 152, for an account of the proofs Campbell gives to support the testimony of the Apostles.

not by some extreme mysticism or with some esoteric faith, but on rational grounds. This attitude of reasonableness, along with other elements of his empirical method, is used to launch his attack on David Hume's treatment of miracles.

Campbell feels that Hume's account and criticism of miracles must be answered. Hume had said that he found it difficult to believe in miracles because he could not believe any testimony that is contrary to universal experience. [21] He maintained that it is more probable that the witnesses were mistaken in their reports than that the laws of nature had been violated. Concerning Hume's position there are two points which Campbell raises: 1) in regard to the "laws of nature"; and 2) in regard to the term "universal experience." Campbell asks how it could be proven that there were "laws of nature" and that these were "inviolable." Do we judge, he asks, a given law of nature to be inviolable by appeal to our own observations through our own senses? Even if we add to our experience that of the observers who formulated these laws on the basis of scientific inquiry, Campbell points out that this constituted, in Hume's time, only half a century of the study of nature. On the basis of this limited experience, to infer, as did Hume, something about the absolute nature of the laws of the universe, is to go far beyond the empirical basis on which philosophy should be grounded. An insufficient attention to the limits of empiricism is Campbell's chief criticism of Hume. [22]

In the second place, Campbell objected to what he calls Hume's speculations about universal experience. He takes Hume to mean that universal experience means the "experience of all persons at all places and at all times," and this, in turn, Campbell judges absurd, for how could one man with his five senses observe the experience of all persons at all places and at all times? All we can know, Campbell retorts, is the experience of one man at one time and in one place, and that is the experience of each individual self. The rest of knowledge is based upon memory or upon faith. By faith, of course, Campbell means here, faith in another person's experience and the reports given of that experience. A single individual can have beliefs about the experiences of other men, perhaps of all men, but an individual can only know directly his own experience. [23] Driving Hume's position to what he regards as a point of absurdity, Campbell accuses Hume of speculation in writing the history of England. Campbell says: "The eloquent author of *The History of England* seems not to have perceived the delusion

21 *Popular Lectures and Addresses,* pp. 154-157.
22 *Ibid.,* p. 118.
23 *Ibid.,* p. 155.

he was imposing upon himself, in making his own individual experience, or that of a few others equal to that of all mankind in all ages of the world, a ten-thousand-millioneth part of which he, nor no other person, ever heard or knew. No man had universal experience, consequently no man could believe it." [24]

The proper context in which to understand Campbell's aversion to Hume is the application of the former's empirical method to religion and morals. Campbell is interested in the establishment of the probability of knowledge which comes from the testimony of others. In order to support his beliefs on religion and morals, one must depend upon the reports contained in the Bible of the experiences of people who lived many centuries ago. As the events recorded in the Bible are inaccessible to any direct observation, this condition necessitates that knowledge of these events of the Bible be built upon a faith in the testimony of those who reported them. Of course, these testimonies must be subjected to the principles of empirical method. Campbell says: "A miracle, indeed, may be a question of fact depending upon human testimony, and so far as it depends upon human testimony, is always credible when that testimony is perfect. On perfect testimony it must be believed, on the principle, that every effect must have an adequate cause. — For should we see a number of persons of sound understanding, radically and essentially change their manner of life, and institute a new course of action, unequivocally contrary to their natural passions and well established habits, submitted to their understanding and their senses, we would be compelled to believe them or, to admit the existence of an effect without a cause." [25]

Hume had maintained that some of the reports given by people in the Bible violate what the rest of humanity has experienced and thus it is likely that the Biblical reporters were mistaken. Thus, Hume's empirical method and criticism of religion and morality appealed to a wider history of man than the reports found in the Scriptures. Campbell, on the other hand, thinks that the appeal to universal human experience is more likely to deceive than the appeal to the observational reports of men in the Bible. Campbell analyzes the issue by claiming that miracles may be contrary to the experience of some men, but not of all men. He relates a story of a Dutch navigator who made the statement that men and horses could pass over water and not sink. The King of Siam ordered the navigator put to death for lying. But the Dutch sailor's experience was different from that of the king; he had lived in the north where iced-over rivers would allow men and horses to cross over

24 *Ibid.*, p. 118.
25 *Protestant Preachers' Companion*, p. 3.

them. The king had never experienced a frozen river, and thus, for him, the navigator's statement was a lie. Using this analogy, Campbell maintains that however contrary miracles are to our experience, they are events in the lives of men, of some men at least, namely, those who experienced such miraculous events in Bible times.

One of the implications of Hume's attack on the possibility of miracles was an aspersion on revealed religion. In order to defend revelation, Campbell argues for the "inspiration" of the Scriptures. He does this by going outside the domain of Christian writers to gather "facts" concerning the credibility of the Scriptures and the truths they attest. He draws upon his vast knowledge of the classical writers to prove his point. He appeals to the writings of Josephus to prove the existence of Jesus and John the Baptist. He compiles an impressive list of authorities to prove belief in the inspiration of the Scriptures: Tacitus, Suetonius, Misha, the Talmud, Pliny, Trajan the emperor, Epictetus, Arrion, Adrian the emperor, Autonius the Pius, Marcus Antonius, Lucian of Samosta, Celsus, Parghry, and Julian the Apostate. [26]

When the miracle of the resurrection of Christ came before Campbell as an issue, he turns his empirical method upon this specific problem in the same way in which he answered Hume on the general nature of miracles. The source of one's belief about the resurrection, of course, is found in the reports in the Bible. But the basis for the acceptance of belief in the event within these reports is founded upon empirical method. Faith in the report and in the testimony must be established. Who saw it? Where and when did they see it? How many saw it and were they reliable witnesses? If, at first, a witness did not believe the event reported or seen, but later came to believe it, the credibility of the report is strengthened. By these criteria the resurrection of Jesus is established, that is, by empirical proof through the testimonies of those who saw and reported the event

There remain two crucial problems which came to the fore in Campbell's religion on the basis of the method by which he worked out his beliefs on revelation, reason, and faith. One of these is the role that the Holy Spirit plays in his view; the other is the function of prayer in the Christian life.

It may be recalled that Campbell lived in a period of American religious history when many heated controversies took place over the operation and role of the Holy Spirit. The revivalism which swept over the new world was often emotionally charged, appealing to the "feelings" rather than to the "intellects" of men. According

26 *Ibid.*, pp. 149-150.

to some religious men of the period, the workings of the Holy Spirit had to condition a person before he could receive the truths of religion.. This view of the Holy Spirit is repugnant to Campbell. On his view, the Spirit is contained in the Word. That is, he believes that the Bible is so plainly written that even the most humble man can receive it into his understanding, and understanding would change his inward nature. Campbell gained the reputation among some of his contemporaries of having a *head* religion, a term denoting his intellectualistic approach to the establishment of religious beliefs. This designation was in contrast to a *heart* religion in which the workings of the Holy Spirit produced emotional manifestations. The relation of the intellect to the emotions in Campbell's thought will be considered later, but it should be noted here that any emotional outburst, religious or otherwise, that is not guided by reason is anathema to Campbell's way of thinking.

Another troublesome aspect of Campbell's religious thought concerns how prayer is to enter into present life. Given the premises that revelation is confined to the Bible and is "a divine communication concerning spiritual and eternal things," how can modern man approach God except through reading the Bible? As Campbell did not believe that God has revealed anything to anyone personally in recent times, how could there be any communication between God and modern man? There are some passages where Campbell seems to speak of prayer as evidence of revelation, but the fuller context of these passages indicates that this communication took place during Biblical times. [27] On the other hand, Campbell gives some glowing accounts of the meaning of prayer following some of the traditional meanings of the term. The Deists, at least some of them, went so far as to maintain that prayer is of no avail. They argued that since God had made the world and set it into operation under mechanical and deterministic laws, it would be foolish to ask God to suspend these laws. It appears that some of the young men who gathered around Campbell took this Deistic position concerning prayer; at least Campbell is criticized by Barton W. Stone for not correcting their views. [28] Be that as it may, it seems that Campbell's views are weak at this point, for, in practice, he did offer prayer and he does think that prayer is a kind of communication with God.

The philosophical and religious theories concerning the roles of revelation, reason, and faith in Campbell's day set the stage upon which the intellectual conflicts were acted out. Campbell lived

---

[27] *Millennial Harbinger*, 1832, p. 110.

[28] *Autobiography of Barton W. Stone* (Cincinnati: J. A. and U. R. James, 1847), p. 76. See the discussion concerning the view that regeneration must take place before understanding.

among these competing philosophies and came to terms with them by selecting some points from each and rejecting others which he deemed unsound. His mind came to rest with an acceptance of the empirical approach to knowledge which was current in his day, with an application of this method as he interpreted it to the Scriptures, with an acceptance of a certain meaning of revelation tempered with the interpretation of the powers and limits of reason, and with a faith which is more practical and logical than private and subjective.

Alexander Campbell stands as an important link in the history of the empirical interpretation of experience, in relation to revealed religion. The impact of the empirical movement upon inherited and derived notions of religious thought has been great, and it has turned religious thinking into many different patterns. To mention only a few: some have taken, as did Campbell in his proofs for the existence of God, sense perception as the basis for inferential statements about what lies beyond what man sees, hears, touches, and feels. What man sees in nature is the work of a Creative God. To others, the movement of empiricism has driven them to make attempts to perceive God directly or to have some kind of direct awareness of His existence. For others, it means that religious symbols have their significance in the emotional life of man, in human feelings, in some kind of experiential aesthetic quality. And for still others, it means that the confrontation of man with sensory impressions contains no religious meaning unless one is driven deeper into his own consciousness to experience the mystery of faith.

Modern day philosophers and religious men might claim that some of Campbell's assumptions about philosophy and religion make his account of experience too narrow; that experience is much broader and deeper, much richer in meaning, than Campbell and the men of the Enlightenment made it. Life is more complex, its processes more complicated, its meanings more extensive. Furthermore, it would be claimed that some of his assumptions lead to absurd conclusions, such as his theory of the origin of language and his views of the source of spiritual ideas. While all this may be true, there is an attitude and a principle which Alexander Campbell propounded again and again and which becomes part of his legacy. It is the principle of restoration. This principle strips away the trivial, goes to the heart of things, emphasizes what is essential. In particular, Campbell applied this principle to the original facts of experience, to the proper function of the church, and to the statement of belief.

When layers of symbols are piled on top of each other to the point that symbols become divorced from original experience, whether Biblical experiences or experiences since Biblical times, there is a need to recover the original and return to primary experience. This is the restoration principles applied to the primacy of fact. When church organizations become so complex with activity piled on top of activity, with meetings and committees and committees and meetings, with hierarchies of authoritative patterns moving up and down the ecclesiastical ladder, then the spirit of Alexander Campbell haunts us to face again and again the problem of the proper meaning of the church. Organizations need to be pruned now and then in order to strip away the non-essential and the trivial. This is the restoration principle applied to the primacy of the church's function. When statements of belief become so expanded that they fill a shelf of volumes requiring a lifetime of reading, then this condition out-credalizes the creeds which Campbell thought were burdensome, and it is time to restore the simplicity of the supreme commitment.

The brooding, probing, agonizing, and prayerful way in which man seeks meaning for life has brought new insights and revelations. Faith sometimes creates its own ideal and believes in it so zealously that the object becomes a fact. This kind of mystical faith has often pushed reason out to the periphery of experience as some kind of demon. On the other hand, some men have gone so far as to enthrone cold, abstract reason to the point that all feelings and emotions are crucified. The legacy of Alexander Campbell is one in which insights and revelations and objects of faith are scrutinized by the proper role of reason so that these matters will not lead to fanaticism. The reasonableness of Campbell's attitude always contains an element of caution; it cautions man that faith might become so private and subjective that it lives upon itself, distorts its own ego, has no connection with other parts of life, and living upon its own fantasies, loses communication even with its God. The restoration principle tempers revelation with reasonableness, controls religious enthusiasm with common sense, and justifies and sobers man's ultimate commitment. In this sense, the restoration principle restores the primacy of a reasonable faith.

IV

GOD, NATURE, AND MAN

The quest for an understanding of the existence and nature of God was no deep and penetrating problem for Alexander Campbell. He seems never to have experienced the kind of soul-searching doubt of the existence of God that a Descartes did. As far as we know, he never entertained any scepticism about the existence of a Supreme Being, for his empirical method, coupled with his views of revelation, reason, and faith made his beliefs about religious matters certain and secure to his own mind. His beliefs about God's existence were formulated on empirical and rational, not emotional, grounds, thus there was no turmoil of mind or of outward demonstrations involved in his commitment.

The concept of God is integral to Campbell's interpretation of life, experience, nature, and of the beginning and end of all things. His idea of God includes not only the existence and nature of God, but also God's relation to nature and God's relation to man. In fact, one of his major works, *The Christian System*, starts with God as the central theme. Primarily he accepted the existence of God on the basis of faith, revelation, and reason, as these terms were interpreted by him. Sometimes he looked to the Scriptures for its revelation and for his faith; sometimes he argued on the basis of reason for the existence of God.

A distinction is usually made between the problem of God's existence on the one hand and the problem of Gods nature or essence on the other. Some thinkers start with the existence of God and derive His nature of essence from His existence; others start with God's essence, or the meaning of the term, and derive His existence from His essence. The relation of God's existence to His essence never confronted Campbell as a problem. He speaks of God's existence and His nature; for instance, in one passage he seems to argue that God's self-existence implies His being infinite, eternal, and immutable; on the other hand, he says that "as we form a character from a man from what he says and what he does, so learn we of the Divine character." [1]

The problem of the essence of God may be put in the form of certain queries. What is God like? What is His nature? What characteristics does God have? What terms can be used in describ-

1 *The Christian System*, p. 20.

ing Him? With respect to the symbols which Campbell applied to God, we find that he follows tradition perhaps more than he realized. At one place he speaks of God in a three-fold way: as Creator, Lawgiver and Redeemer. Because of these three functions of God, certain descriptive terms are applied to Him. As Creator, God is "wisdom, power, and goodness." As Lawgiver, He is "justice, truth, and holiness." As Redeemer, God is "mercy, condescension, and love." [2] Campbell says that the Scriptures speak of God's divinity, of His "Godhead," as well as of "the unity, spirituality, and eternity of His being." Campbell thought that all these terms are ascertained from reading the Bible.

The problem of the relations within God Himself appear to Campbell as a kind of insoluble problem. It will be recalled that Campbell indicated several parts of God's nature, for instance, intellect and will. The mind or intellect of God contains "archetypes" of ideas out of which the world is fashioned. Like many religious thinkers before him, Campbell claims that the "archetypes" of ideas in God's mind do not have the power to reproduce themselves in the actual world of nature and of man. God's will, guided by His intellect, creates the world. But troublesome problems arise for him, as he admitted, when he tries to deal with the "holy and incomprehensible relations in the Divinity." [3] This involves the problem of the "trinity," although Campbell did not like that designation.

The manner in which Campbell treats of the various constituents within the divinity starts with "God" and the "Spirit of God." Each of these is capable of a separate and distinct existence, although Campbell does not know how this can be the case. At any rate, he claims that it is the "Spirit of God" which is the active agent, responsible for "all divine perfections and works." Furthermore, it is this operative agent which makes the new creation and makes for the "holiness" of Christians. It is this spirit which pervades the church, which is the "body" with Jesus as the "head." Terms like the "Son of God" belong to the man Jesus, the man born during the days of Augustus Caesar; but the Word which is incarnate is "the person called our Lord and Redeemer, Jesus Christ." Campbell can say without any qualification of his doctrine that we have "the Father, Son, and Holy Spirit equally divine, though personally distinct from each another." [4] The best way that Campbell can treat this difficult problem is by appeal to analogy. He argues from the personal manifestation in man to the plurality of the personal manifestation in God. But in the final analysis, Campbell admits that the whole problem of the relation of the

2 *Ibid.,* p. 20.
3 *Ibid.,* p. 26.
4 *Ibid.,* p. 21.

various constituents within God's nature is incomprehensible to man's mind. Campbell's humility before such a problem is admitted, as he says: "for — who, by searching can find out God, or know the Almighty to perfection? The knowledge of Him is high as heaven. What canst thou do? deeper than hell, what canst thou know? The measure thereof is longer than the earth, and broader than the sea." [5]

On the relation of God to nature and to man, Campbell puts forth a religious philosophy which is based upon the notion of God as Creator and that the universe or nature exists because He created it. It should be noted, too, that God is not found in nature, but the Spirit of God is the animating element of nature. The relation of God to nature and to man is partly explained in Campbell's description of the various stages of revelation found in the Bible. In the first stage of man's existence, the state of Edenic purity, man knew God directly. The relationship between God and man was so intimate that no "self-disclosure" of God was necessary. But with the Fall, a new dimension entered man's experience. The withdrawal of God from the world and from man in this aspect of Campbell's view does not mean that withdrawal was complete and final. From time to time, God revealed Himself to man in Biblical history after the Fall.

On the matter of the existence of cosmic evil, that is, the evil which exists in nature, and not the evil which enters experience through the errors and mistakes of man's decisions, Campbell takes a position which leaves the problem of cosmic evil in obscurity. He says that "we may conjecture much, but can know little of the origin of moral evil in God's dominion." [6] The faith he shares with others in the age of the Enlightenment concerning the goodness that is in nature was expressed in this passage: "It is not necessary that we should analyze and comprehend the origin of darkness in order to enjoy the light of the sun." [7] The conclusion that can be drawn here is that God's world which He created and fashioned in some way out of his wisdom and goodness is a good world on the whole, even if some parts of it are not fully understood. Evil is admitted to be an actual fact, but there is "as much good as Almighty power can achieve." [8]

The foregoing analysis of Campbell's view of the existence and nature of God forms the central theme of what he called *The Christian System*. Other parts of that system are found in his view of cosmology, or the view of nature, and in his view of man.

5 *Ibid.,* p. 20.
6 *Ibid.,* p. 31.
7 *Ibid.,* p. 31.
8 *Ibid.,* p. 31.

When Campbell attended the University of Glasgow, he took a course in Experimental Philosophy. The title of the course is descriptive of the new view of nature which had been popularized by Francis Bacon, who is sometimes called the father of modern science. Forerunners of Bacon had suffered at the hands of intellectual reactionaries who attempted to stamp out the new science, but by the time Bacon appeared on the scientific and philosophic scene, enough minds were tolerant of new ideas to allow some communication about them. By the time Campbell came to Glasgow, Thomas Reid, foremost spokesman for the new philosophy in the University, had written to a generation before: "Wise men now agree, or ought to agree, in this, that there is but one way to knowledge of nature's works — the way of observation and experiment." [9] Sixteen years after Bacon's death, Sir Isaac Newton was born, and the importance of Newton's principles and methods is noted by Reid: "The man who first discovered that cold freezes water, and that heat turns it into vapour, proceeded on the same general principles, and in the same method by which Newton discovered the law of gravitation and the properties of light." [10] These statements by Reid are cited to illustrate one significant point: observation and experiment had gained acceptance in the minds of scholars after the long years of bitter controversy.

It has already been noted in another instance how Campbell adopts Bacon's method of induction and uses it in heaping fact upon fact for the establishment of belief about some Biblical event or for the settlement of a doctrinal point by enumeration of the various usages of a word. The method of induction did not, of course, originate in Biblical studies; it first appeared in scientific pursuits and Campbell adopted the method and applied it to his empirical approach to the Scriptures. But the belief in the method of induction was so engrained in the scholars at Glasgow that Thomas Reid placed this "propensity" to generalize in the very constitution of man. He wrote: "By our constitution, we have a strong propensity to trace particular facts and observations to general rules, and to apply such general rules to account for other effects, or to direct us in the production of them. This procedure of the understanding is familiar to every human creature in the common affairs of life, and it is the only one by which any real discovery in philosophy can be made." [11] Thus, this method of scientific study turned upon natural objects was so honored and popular that even before Campbell went to the university, men like Reid and others would read its procedure into the psychology of the human race.

9 G. A. Johnston, ed., *Selections from the Scottish Philosophy of Common Sense* (Chicago: The Open Court Publishing Co., 1915), p. 26.
10 *Ibid.*, pp. 28-29.
11 *Ibid.*, p. 28.

Newton showed by his methods and principles that the universe is something like a machine; that is, operations are simple and invariant, predictable, and apparently universal. Starting with minute data, hypotheses and theories can be formulated which are then extended to new data, and this procedure can go on and on until we conceive a whole system to which all the theories apply. Of course, the application of any theory to new data is constantly checked and verified by observation. One of the significant implications for philosophy and religion which Newton drew from his studies was a picture of nature as having a purposive and harmonious arrangement, and this, he thought, proved the existence of God. In Newton's view, the system of nature is governed by rigid laws; the scientific mind constructs its theories by applying these laws to part after part until the entire system is complete. What Newton did was to bind together "in one dazzling synthesis the great and the little, the stars in their courses and the fall of an apple." [12]

Campbell's approach to cosmology or his view of nature is decidedly Newtonian. It breathes the atmosphere of Newtonian science, and if not stemming directly from Newton himself, certainly is an echo of the Newtonian theme. Campbell was born just fifty-one years after the death of Newton, but Newton's *Principia* had been in circulation since 1687. For Campbell, the universe is a system of systems. His conception of the systematic nature of the universe runs all the way from the stars to inorganic life. Such a universe might be called, in his own words, "a chain of systems," for all the systems that make up the universe are but component parts of it. Campbell's recourse to the human being itself throws some light on his view of how the part of a system is connected to a whole. He says, for instance, "in the person of a single, individual man, we have an animal system, an intellectual system, a moral system, running into each other, and connecting themselves with every thing of a kindred nature in the whole universe of God, just as we have in the human body itself a system of solids and a system of fluids, these again forming themselves into a system of bones, a system of nerves, a system of arteries, a system of veins, etc." [13] It must be understood that Campbell's view of the various "systems" of nature is not something which is determined *a priori*, that is, prior to experience and observation. Thus, he claims that such systems cannot be understood abstractly, but must be observed in the same empirical way as he maintained other things are observed. The study of these particular systems must be undertaken in

12 Basil Willey, *The Eighteenth Century Background* (New York: Columbia University Press, 1953). See especially the chapter on "The Turn of the Century," pp. 1-26.
13 *The Christian System*, p. 13.

reference to "that system which is proximate to it in nature and use." [14] A case in point is the example of the human body mentioned in the preceding sentences; an observational study must be made of the constitution of the human body and of the connections of bones and muscles.

Since the systems of the universe run into each other, they do not stand alone and isolated, but as the systems are interdependent, knowledge "about" such systems is interdependent too. Now, if this is the case in Campbell's view of nature, then our knowledge of any system is necessarily tied to knowledge of the systems to which it is proximately or even remotely related. Campbell's view of nature and of the knowledge about it has some far reaching implications. Campbell sees, for instance, that it would be a "mark of imbecility of mind" for anyone to dogmatize with an air of infallibility or assume the attitude of perfect intelligence on any one subject of human thought without an intimate knowledge of the entire system of nature. One of the consequences of this position is that one cannot understand one atom of the universe without understanding all of it. This view of nature and of the knowledge appropriate to it means for Campbell that all of our conclusions must be tentative, and we must admit that our knowledge is always partial and incomplete.

Dugald Stewart, a Scottish common-sense realist whom Campbell called "the greatest of all metaphysicians," had maintained that the work of the scientist and the philosopher is that of analysis and synthesis. [15] Campbell follows this method of thinking. He believes, as did Stewart, that man can divide the "mighty whole" of the universe into smaller parts for the purpose of study. The method of analysis, of breaking up the larger wholes into smaller units, makes the complexities of the universe come under easy intellectual management. If man starts with the solar systems, he can divide these into separate solar systems; each solar system can then be divided into planets, both primary and secondary. Then the division can be moved down to the various kingdoms: mineral, vegetable, animal, and intellectual. Again, these "kingdoms" or systems can be divided into genera, species, and individuals, until the single individual becomes the proper and distinct theme of study. But even the individual within a species may be too large for appropriate study. So, the individual is broken into further divisions, such as the primary elements of its nature, its attributes, modes, and circumstances of its existence. This is the only way that Campbell thinks the complexities of nature can come within "easy grasp of a special operation of our minds."

14 *Ibid.*, p. 13.
15 Johnston, *Selections from the Scottish Philosophy of Common Sense*, p. 232.

Empirical method as presented by Campbell makes the individual the focus of study. In philosophical language, Campbell follows what developed in his times as the philosophy of "nominalism." Nominalism holds that only the individual is "real," or at least primary in existence and knowledge; that is, abstractions and generalizations referring to classes or the systems of the universe must be treated as ways of speaking of or referring to real entities. The universe thus presents itself, as Campbell conceives it, not in the abstract, but in the concrete. This is the nominalist position. At the same time, all these various individuals which compose the universe are related, or as he says, there is not a single thing existing alone and isolated in the entire universe. There can be no doubt that this position held by Campbell on the matter of individuals being the most real things that exist has important implications for his philosophy as a whole. For instance, starting with individuals, the empiricist keeps close to the "facts" of observation and does not get lost in abstractions. Parenthetically, we might add that "the church" on this philosophic position is not an abstract entity; it is each specific and individual church which is concrete and real. However, on this philosophy, this does not mean that churches as individual units are not related to each other; on the general principles of philosophy put forth by Campbell, no single or individual church can stand alone and isolated. Each individual church must be understood in relation to other churches or in a system of churches. The same philosophy applies to individual man. It is true that the individual man is important; each is a concrete entity and has a real existence. But individuals are related to each other and form a system. Theories and laws, such as those constructed by Newton, can express these relations. The falling of an apple is a specific, individual event, but this event cannot be understood isolated and alone from other events of its kind; it must be related in a system of law. The connecting links between and among individuals form systems, and the systematization of the universe is the work of synthesis.

The approach which Campbell makes to nature requires something of the mind of man who seeks to understand it. Man must approach the whole of nature with caution, modesty, and humility, for the universe has a vastness to it which the feeble mind of man finds difficult to grasp. In Campbell's words: "Who could pronounce upon the wisdom and utility of a single joint, without an understanding of the body to which it ministers; of that world in which it moves and of the relations which it sustains; of that world without some acquaintance with the solar system of which it is but a small part; of that particular solar system without a general and even intimate knowledge of all the kindred systems; of all these kindred systems without a through comprehension of the ultimate design of the whole creation; of that ultimate design, without a perfect intelli-

gence of that incomprehensible. Being by whom and for whom all
things were created and made."[16] Nature is so large, so vast in its
complexities that Campbell thinks the science of his day had not
explored all of it. In fact, he uses this argument against David Hume
when the latter thought he could speak of the "universality of experience." Campbell thinks Hume had made a "hasty generalization"
about the nature of the universe. Thus, what are called miracles
might be brought within the bounds of reason if we knew more
about nature itself.

There is an aspect of Campbell's view of nature which is related
to his theory of knowledge, but which, as was noted in another
context, is not fully developed. Locke had maintained that each
species of nature had an "archetype" or general pattern which somehow determined each of the classes or species which make up
nature. Campbell held to a theory of "archetypes" as well, and when
this part of his theory of knowledge is brought into conjunction with
his theory of nature, it can be seen that he, too, means that each
class or species in nature has an archetype. There is a theoretical
impasse in his view of knowledge and of nature, however, when he
maintains that all the individuals in nature are related in systems, but
at the same time the archetypes which make up the "models" of the
classes or species in nature are "independent" of each other. How
can the models be self-sufficient and independent when their coun-
terparts in the empirical world are ordered in a system of systems?
This part of his philosophy of nature and of the knowledge appropriate to it is undeveloped.

It is doubtful that one can find a man of religion in the day in
which Campbell lived who was more thoroughly modern in his
views of science and of nature. He shares the attitude of the age in
being anti-speculative in natural things, and he relegated to the
realm of "speculative" the whole paraphernalia of "substances" and
"essences." [17] He even goes so far as to maintain that the "essence"
of mind and matter are completely shut off from the understanding
of man. His acceptance of Newtonian science with the peculiar bent
of the age which made observation of concrete individuals the chief
emphasis is noteworthy. His view of analysis and synthesis applied
to observable things, and his extreme caution about generalizing
with any kind of dogmatism are a credit to his sensitive mind. His
reasonableness about all things in nature, human history, and
especially religious events are significant insights and show the
modernity of his mind.

Furthermore, there is no conflict in Campbell's mind about the
acceptance of the best science of his day and the older beliefs

16 *The Christian System*, p. 14.
17 Campbell shows his indebtedness to both the Renaissance and to the
Enlightenment on this problem. See *Popular Lectures and Addresses*, p. 75.

about the world which had been such a pitfall for many another religious thinker. Campbell accepts the modern view of solar systems, with suns as centers of these systems; thus, he was completely Copernican in his astronomical views. He accepts the fact that the world of nature is made up of "form" and "matter" as its two basic constituents; thus, there is no conflict over the problem of "materialism" in physics. In this respect, he accepts the new physics of his day, the physics of Newton, and these are parts of his own philosophy of nature. It should be noted too, that nature, for Campbell, is not something to be abhorred, or feared, or held in disrespect. Nature is something to be loved and cherished; it is something that stirs the wonderment of the human mind; it is something that sustains the human body. Above all else, this world of nature is something for human beings to take delight in, for after all, God made this world for man to take pleasure in and to enjoy.

In his analysis of the nature of man, Campbell makes his basic divisions of the parts or aspects of man's nature on the grounds of a linguistic approach to the problem. He thinks that man is composed of three main parts, namely, body, soul, and spirit. [18] It is by appeal to the languages of the Greeks, the Romans, and the English that he begins his description, as all three make divisions in their speech concerning man's nature. The Greek names for these parts are *soma, psyche,* and *pneuma;* the Latin names are *corpus, anima,* and *spiritus.* The English call them *body, soul,* and *spirit.* Campbell's analysis is closer to the Greeks when he maintains that horses and dogs have a soul or life; in fact, every creature "from the mammoth to the veriest animalcule" has an *anima,* or soul or life. But horse, dogs, and animalcules do not have a *pneuma* or spirit. Man, of course, has a body and a soul, as do the animals, but man is not a mere vegetable or mere animal. Campbell recognizes that the line of difference between men and animals is not always easily determined where intelligence is concerned, although it is only fair to say that generally he holds, as have all thinkers, that the intellectual powers are more highly developed in man. The distinguishing characteristic of man which sets him off from vegetables and animals is man's possession of a spirit. The spirit of man sets him off from the rest of the world and "places his life first among the sacred things of creation."

In Campbell's philosophy, the body, soul, and spirit of man are separate and discrete parts, and no two of these are identical, thus, the soul cannot be equated with spirit, or the spirit with body. Of course, this position poses a deep psychological and philosophical

18 *Popular Lectures and Addresses,* p. 293

problem which seems never to have bothered Campbell, as well as other thinkers of the Enlightenment. What is the relation of the "spirit" to the "body"? How do these two separate entities, or if they are not designated as "entities," these two discrete parts of man's nature interact? About all that can be made of Campbell's view is that somehow spirit does influence the body, and somehow the body, particularly through its appetites and passions, exerts some influence upon the spirit.

Campbell thinks that it is through *consciousness* that man discovers that he has a *will*. [19] The will is the whole mind in action to effect a change in some person or thing. The proof for the existence of such a will is founded upon the contention that all rational beings feel conscious, and as they feel this consciousness they act upon the presumption that the mind is a self-moving principle or that it has the power of originating its own volitions. The consciousness of a will in man is so immediate and so indubitable that to deny it would be analogous to trying to tell a man that he did not have a toothache when he himself felt the "exquisite twinges." It is when the operation or function of the will is brought into conjunction with other parts of man's psychological make-up that Campbell's analysis becomes complex. The primary powers of the human mind — perception, memory, and consciousness — are of such a nature that the will has no power whatsoever over them. For instance, we may have perceptions contrary to our volitions — these perceptions are simply "there" in our experience and there is nothing we can do about it. The same is true of memory, as experiences written upon the "table of memory" brought forth by some singular associations will involuntarily present themselves to our minds in a vivid manner irrespective of our wishes. Consciousness, as well, like the consciousness of our thought life, depends not upon any act of the will, but upon "the constitution of the mind itself." [20] Sensations are also beyond the control of will, as simple ideas are forced upon us by the very nature of our experience.

The human will, however, can exercise certain powers and can control certain acts. When we examine the operations of the mind and take cognizance of the "faculties" of recollecting, reflecting, imagining, reasoning, and judging, we discover that these faculties are under the control of the will or of volition. Campbell uses the faculties of imagination and of reasoning to make his point. We observe that in exercising the faculty of imagination we can transfer the characteristics or qualities, or as he calls them, "the external

19 *Campbell-Owen Debate,* I, pp. 142-143.
20 *Ibid.,* I, p. 143.

peculiarities," of one animal to the body of another and thus create any kind of imagined monster. We can do this transferring of some characteristic from one animal to another "at will," thus, the act of imagination is under the control of volition. What holds for the act of imagination also holds for the act of memory, for Campbell holds that recollection comes by making an effort, and the determination of the effort to remember is under our control. In the same manner, he maintains that we can reason only when we "decide" to reason; and we can perform the act of judging in much the same way as by previous determination we decide to eat supper or go to bed. [21] Some bodily functions can be classified under the category of voluntary operations while others must be regarded as involuntary. For instance, man can move his eyes, hands, and feet by an act of the will; but man cannot move his heart, his lungs, or liver and continue to live.

The foregoing discussion of the nature of the will as the action of the whole mind and of the relation of the will to different parts of the mind leads to a more philosophical determination of voluntary and involuntary actions. This is the problem of freedom and determinism. On this problem Campbell does not choose to use the term "free agent"; rather, he thought the term "rational agent" would better fit the nature of man. The reason given for this distinction is that freedom means for him "the self-determining power of the mind" and it is not to be made analogous to such expressions as we might use in ordinary speech when we say, "free as running water" or "free as the blowing of the wind." The notion that man is a "rational agent," not a free agent, is derived from observation, experience, and from reason itself. Thus, man can act sometimes by the self-determining power in his own mind, sometimes under the dominance of the influence of circumstance.

Some implications of Campbell's view of man's volitional powers extend into his notion of the act of *believing*. He shows that a man cannot believe at will, for belief is conditional upon having evidence. The notion that beliefs are forged out of voluntary actions but guided by evidence is integral to his approach to religious matters. That is why one needs the "facts" of the Bible to "compel" belief; for it as absurd to hold that anyone can believe without evidence as it is to maintain that one can see without light. Now, one cannot always determine *what* the object presents as a candidate for belief or *when* he sees or believes, but it should not be overlooked that both seeing and believing are completely out of the control of volition. We may voluntarily seek

21 *Ibid.*, p. 143.

to inquire or to investigate a belief or an object which we see, and this experience may be guided by duty, curiosity, and interest. If interpretation be allowed on this point, it may be said that one may "will" or voluntarily decide to read the Bible, although he cannot "will" that certain things be found there. One cannot change what he sees or reads, but he can choose to look or to read. But Campbell believes that the facts of the Bible are so compelling that if one does choose to read it, then his belief would be compelled.

Campbell does not believe that man acts without a "motive," for to maintain such a view, he thinks, would be the same as holding that man acts irrationally or without reason. He means here that the "deliberative" side of man's life is under control of motive and reason. And he does not want such voluntary, rational determination to be interpreted as "necessity," for this would mean that man would be exempted from all blame and praise. Praise and blame are appropriate when man has deliberately and voluntarily decided to perform an act. Over these acts of man reason sits in judgment, condemning man when he acts irrationally and approving and acquitting him when he acts rationally. But a further problem arises as to the explanation of how man acts irrationally, whether through deliberation or not. Here, Campbell brings in the role that passions and appetites play in the control of the will. There is a kind of internal war in man when the rational motives come into conflict with the appetites and passions for the direction of action.

Thus far consideration of Campbell's view of man has centered upon his broad view of human nature and upon the specific operations of the mind. A much deeper problem is involved in his view of man as an individual being, or as he called it, the problem of "personal identity." This problem may be put in a series of questions: How does one know that he is the same "person" today as he was yesterday? As man's body may change considerably during a lifetime, how does one know that the same "spirit" or "soul" resides in it? Campbell's treatment of this problem is similar to Locke's; both make a distinction between the "man" and the "person." The man may change, but substantially the person remains the same person amid the changes. Campbell holds that man is an "ego," and again using the linguistic opproach, he says that we attach the terms "me" and "mine" to this ego. But the most descriptive term for this notion of the ego is the pronoun "I." The "I" is the pronoun, he says, which has no gender, number, or case. Our languages take the meaning of the "ego" and the "I" to be representative of "one personality," and personality, for Campbell, is "one body, soul, spirit acting in one corporation, constituting

one substantive pronoun and one human person." [22]   Campbell
appears to make a distinction between the person and the man,
as did Locke, for he maintains that the human person, "the pro-
nominal I," may live, move and have its proper being and individuality in ten bodies during one lifetime. This analysis attempts
to show that the "man" or the body part of man may change, yet
there remains a "personal identity" through these changes. Another
way Campbell has of putting this idea of man's "substantial"
permanence amid his transitory changes is that the same person
may inhabit various houses during his lifetime, and figuratively
speaking, the man may lose a room or some of its furniture, like
an arm, or a limb, or both arms and a limb — and yet the personality, the personal identity, the "consciousness" of his thinking,
willing, acting "I" remains the same.

If man's body changes, what about his spirit? It has been
shown that personal identity is located in the mind or the spirit
of man, as in his consciousness, or as it is sometimes termed, his
"self-consciousness." Does the spirit of man change, or is it immutable, permanent? Again, Campbell holds views similar to Locke;
both hold that the "consciousness" and the "spirit" of man changes
and yet it is this consciousness or spirit which constitutes the
substantial person, an ego or "I" which pervades all the changes
of the body. Campbell holds that the spirit of man is "transformable
by intellectual, moral, and spiritual considerations, arguments, and
motives." Hence it is possible that while man's body is changing
in the course of a lifetime, his spirit may be changing too. On the
other hand, Campbell holds that the spirit of man is a positive
entity, or a positive ego. Furthermore, the spirit of man is not a
mode of some other substance or being, such as an attribute or a
quality of a substance. The spirit of man is an individual entity;
it does not arise out of association with others. If the spirit of man
changes, then it is this individual entity which changes. Proof that
the spirit of man can and does change is given by Campbell in
the fact that this spirit can become defiled and become a monster. [23]

Campbell has a problem of uniting some of the basic assumptions concerning man which he adopted from the Enlightenment
thinkers and some of his inherited beliefs about man's evil nature
as held in traditional religion. The manner in which he attempts to
combine these two dialectically opposed views of man's nature is
not always convincing, but his attempt is interesting. In the first
place, Campbell accepts the Biblical view described before that
man at one time lived in the state of Edenic purity. In this state

22 *Popular Lectures and Addresses,* p. 294.
23 *The Christian System,* p. 29.

man was not sinful and he did not have the consciousness of sin. There was no evil in the universe or in man. Sin entered the human race when man disobeyed the commandments of God. [24] Thus, Campbell accepts the Biblical account of the corruption of human nature, at least in the historical sense of that account. But how this corruption is passed on from generation to generation or how it arises in individual man is not always clear in his account of the nature of man; that is, his religious account gives way to a philosophical account of the origin of evil.

Campbell holds, as have many philosophers, that the moral powers of man are more imperfect by nature than man's physical and intellectual powers. The reason given for this position is that the ways by which men can go wrong in matters of moral decision stem more from the nature of such a decision itself as well as the ever-changing character of the objects and activities upon which the decision is made. Man is susceptible to fluctuations in his passions and appetites and these constantly compete for power over the will with the rational powers. A weak character succumbs to the lures of these appetites and passions and gradually by decision making and habit becomes defiled. In Campbell's version of how evil enters into human nature, the burden of responsibility is placed squarely upon man himself in the decisions he makes about the objects he desires and the activities he chooses.

Campbell does hold the view that Christ was sent to earth for the "expiation" of sin. [25] But the manner in which he interpreted this point has a uniqueness about it not usually found among religious thinkers. The means by which man comes to salvation is from examining the Scriptures, which he understands, of course, as the New Testament, which is beyond the Law of the Old Testament. When man opens his eyes to the Scriptures, reads the words written there, and believes on the evidence presented, then he is delivered from sin. Man's spirit is thus changed by the working of the Word upon it, but for the most part the matter of conversion is a highly intellectual process.

As the universe is willed by a benevolent God, Campbell thinks that this universe is created upon a principle which favors virtue and punishes vice. This principle of favoring and punishing seems to apply more to man's life here and now. Campbell does hold there is a heaven and a hell; these words he found in the Bible. But the more important matters of a Christian character and life upon earth concerned him more. Even when he does treat of heaven or hell, it is not always clear whether he considers these as places,

24 *Ibid.,* p. 27.
25 *Ibid.,* p. 39.

conditions, or moral states. [26] The existence of heaven, hell, and immortality are "facts" found in the Bible, and the Biblical report seems all that is required for him to believe in them.

When one reviews the famous debate Campbell had with Robert Owen, he is struck by how much attention each man places upon an analysis of the nature of man. Each man adopted different premisses concerning human nature and rode off in different directions. Throughout the debate, Campbell attempted to show that man cannot reach his highest fulfillment without knowledge of the Bible. It is through the Bible that man learns of the principles which help him achieve the supreme state of blessedness. On the philosophical side, the views of Campbell and Owen are similar in many respects, as the nature of their analyses of sensory knowledge, and the roles of choice, reason, and habit show. But on Campbell's view, man is devoid of the most important beliefs, religious and moral, if he does not accept the Bible as the Revealed Word of God.

Campbell's account of the nature and destiny of man, like that of others of the Enlightenment who made similar assumptions, has its merits and its limitations. His attempt to wed the starting place of his empiricism, especially the view that a child is born with a mind that is a blank tablet, with the views of man he found in the Bible is a valiant undertaking. Viewed from the standpoint of subsequent history, Campbell must be placed within the modern temper, with those thinkers who are on the scientific side of the great divide which Locke instituted between the old and new account of human psychology and philosophy. But the subsequent history of man's experience has driven empiricism much deeper into the nature of human life. Experience is fuller, deeper, richer, more paradoxical and tragic, than Campbell and the men of the Enlightenment understood. Since Campbell's day, man has lived through triumph and defeat; he has suffered, bled, and died. He has fought for his ideals through blood, sweat, and tears. He has undergone elation and despair; at times he is jubilant and optimistic, and at other times he is melancholy to the point of a sickness unto death. Man has inflicted hurt and he has been hurt; he has been brutal and brutalized. He has experienced a dreadful freedom and he has felt that everywhere he is in chains. In recent times, a more realistic empiricism has corrected the overwhelming faith which Campbell and the men of the Enlightenment had in human nature.

And yet, there is a kind of valiant optimism about Campbell's philosophy and religion which is admirable. He was secure in his

26 See the entire essay entitled, "Life and Death," in *Popular Lectures and Addresses*, pp. 403-452.

beliefs about God, about God's goodness, about the good universe which he thought God had created, and about the scientific venture and all it held for man's understanding and enjoyment. He was not entirely oblivious that men could become evil, but he believed steadfastly in the possibilities of human achievement. Confident in His God, in the nature which nurtured and sustained human life, and in the reasonableness of his fellows, Alexander Campbell set forth in his life, like Walt Whitman's voyager, to seek and to find. And what he found was a science, a philosophy, and a religious outlook which became convincing and satisfying to millions of his American followers.

V

ETHICS, POLITICS, AND EDUCATION

Alexander Campbell thinks that man is different from other animals and possesses a spirit which gives him a peculiar sacredness. God made man in His own image and gave him power and dominion over the earth. Man is by nature a moral being because he has the power to choose between alternatives set before him in the situations he encounters. The moral life, says Campbell, involves an understanding of the origin, nature, the relations, the obligations, and the destiny of man. [1] According to Campbell, man is free to map out courses of action and to retract from them if the consequences are painful and to pursue them again if the consequences are pleasing. There is implied here a view which may be called the "pleasure and pain principle," and it will be seen how this principle is united with his view of moral principles given by revealed religion. First, let us look at Campbell's description of general moral behavior.

Freedom of choice among alternatives cannot, of course, be irresponsible, for if choice is irresponsible, then it is immoral. Furthermore, the concepts of responsibility and irresponsibility involve some view of the social nature of man. When Campbell's nominalism is applied to human beings, it results in an "individualism," but it is not an individualism which isolates one individual from other individuals in the universe. From the analogy of the moral with the physical world, Campbell drew some interesting conclusions. In the design of the physical world, the central masses are the largest in their respective systems and they are the "radiating centers" to those systems. Thus, when observation and analysis is turned upon the physical world, the conclusion to be drawn from these operations yields a view that there is a universal law that "minors must be subject to their majors" or that "inferior masses" shall depend upon the superior. The consequences of this analogical thinking in the moral world is that there are mental inequalities in human beings; that all men are not equal by nature, education, or art.

Inequality is, then, one of the basic constituents or generic traits of the universe as Campbell conceives it. The implications he develops out of this concept are many, but he draws out most

[1] *Popular Lectures and Addresses,* p. 99.

of them in regard to art and morality. For he holds that the "beauty" as well as the "happiness" of the universe required such inequality running through all of God's creation. Thus, he claims that "equal lines, smooth surfaces, and eternal plains have no beauty." He goes on to say: "We must have hill and dale, mountain and valley, sea and land, suns of all magnitudes, worlds of all sizes, minds of all dimensions, and persons and faces of diverse casts and colors, to constitute a beautiful and happy world." [2] Now, this poetic passage does point up the variety which makes up the world, but there is an implication in it which ties Campbell to an old tradition when it comes to the moral life. Aristotle had maintained many centuries ago, and the idea has been perpetuated by many who make a case for benevolence, that society needs the poor and the rich in order that the rich may practice charity toward the poor. Note how Campbell's treatment on this point reads: "The world needs the rich and the poor — the young and the aged — the learned and the unlearned — the healthy and the infirm — and the cheerful and the melancholic." [3] Such inequalities, he maintained, "furnish the opportunities for communicating and receiving benefits."

From this notion of the inequalities of human life and the view that all individuals in the universe, atoms as well as men, are interconnected, Campbell's view of responsibility is built. There is "not one lawless atom in the universe," he claims, and by analogy he holds that there is "not one irresponsible agent in the social system." "The doctrine of responsibility," he writes, "is the doctrine of moral relations between an inferior and a superior, between an independent and dependent being; as well as between coordinates as enter into any social compact implying and involving obligations to each other." [4] There are many implications in what Campbell says here, but he left most of them undeveloped. Note that he speaks of the compacts between equals and the obligations entailed, but for the most part, he never expanded upon this important idea. Furthermore, implied in his view of the inequalities of human beings is a justification of benevolence, but again, he simply takes benevolence for granted as a Christian virtue and never gives any other justification for it. [5]

It was quite common in the philosophical climate of Campbell's day for moral philosophers to claim that man has some implanted "moral sense." This moral sense is inferred probably from the fact that man can choose between the better and the worse, between

2 *Popular Lectures and Addresses*, p. 80.
3 *Ibid.*, p. 80.
4 *Ibid.*, p. 78.
5 Benevolence is commanded by the Scriptures and has consequences of pleasure both to the giver and to the receiver.

good and evil. In Campbell's thought, the moral sense is assumed and equated with "conscience," but beyond this, he gave little attention to it. In one passage, he says: "The moral sense or conscience is that power which, when properly educated, dictates and appreciates the character of actions, as they affect and bear upon the persons, the property and character of our neighbors and fellow-citizens. Religion sanctions these, but religion properly indicates our duties to God." [6] The moral sense must be educated in order to detect what is better and worse, good and bad.

It has been indicated that Campbell holds to a "pleasure and pain principle" in moral behavior, that there is "retraction when the pain of the consequences is unpleasing and seeking again the same kind of object when the pleasure of the consequences is pleasing." Memory plays a role in such experiences, for memory tells us what objects have been pleasurable and which have been painful in the past. What man *should* seek is a goal or an object which has pleasure associated with it. The ultimate criterion of any object or human striving for a goal is human happiness or bliss.

But pleasures are not all on the same level of worth. Campbell says that the pleasures of the senses are the lowest form of human happiness. He condemns that philosophy which maintains that all man should seek is to eat, drink, and be merry, which is an extreme type of hedonism (pleasure) and not the central part of the philosophical doctrine. On the other hand, Campbell is not an "ascetic" or one who thinks that man should avoid sensory or bodily pleasures of all kinds. In fact, the whole universe was created by God for our enjoyment, but he places some pleasures on a higher scale of value than others. For instance, Campbell holds that the "intellectual" pleasures of man are superior to those of bodily appetites. [7] Man's superior thrill comes from his "power to apprehend and to understand the magnificence of all creation." The desire for knowledge, he thinks, is an innate craving of every human being. This innate desire is found as assuredly in a child when the child delights in his desire for knowledge as in the animal where its exerts itself to find relief from something which is irritating its body. The natural curiosity of a child to know drives its mind into the pursuit of new ideas. The intellectual pleasure which follows upon this experience becomes cumulative. Campbell describes the thrill of this knowing process: "The ineffable pleasure of the first conception only invites the second effort; and success in that, stimulates the third; and so on, in increasing ratios, until the full-grown man, on his full-fledged wings of intellectual maturity, soars aloft." [8]

6 *Popular Lectures and Addresses*, p. 303.
7 *Ibid.*, p. 91.
8 *Ibid.*, p. 96.

The world is so constituted by God that man's intellectual pleasures are possible. For the world has a variety of objects, and it is from intellectual apprehension of these that man obtains new pleasures. The multitudinous variety of objects and the new ideas which it is possible to derive from them sets the stage for man's "unquenchable thirst" for knowledge. As there is always something new to know and even in a full lifetime man can never learn it all, then the intellectual pleasures are limitless.

Although intellectual pleasures are superior to the bodily pleasures, the former are not the highest in man's accomplishment of happiness. Moral powers are superior to the intellectual and bodily powers, but none of these stand in sharp opposition to each other. Campbell says that the animal pleasures are positive, but not as high as the intellectual pleasures; the moral pleasure is the highest degree of human bliss. [9] But the moral achievement is the hardest to come by, for the moral powers of man are more imperfect by nature than the physical and intellectual powers. The reason for this is that the objects upon which the moral powers operate are peculiar in nature and ever-changing in character. Furthermore, the moral powers are more unfit for discrimination and guidance than are the physical and intellectual powers. For this reason the cultivation and education of the moral powers becomes difficult. It is not the possession of any capacity or power but the creative exercise of it which affords either utility or pleasure to ourselves and others. Man possesses by nature moral powers just as he possesses a body and for that fact alone he cannot be praised or blamed. But when he exercises these powers in "acts" of choice which affect society and which are guided by religious and moral feeling and by reason, then he may make himself and others happy.[10]

Campbell thinks it regrettable that common opinion holds intellectual worth to be more important than moral worth. People, he says, are proud of their children when they display extraordinary intellectual powers, but they do not have this same feeling of pride in their children's advance in moral behavior. In the same manner in which he develops his faculty psychology, he claims that the development of the intellectual powers does not necessarily develop the moral powers. Moral improvement, like all the other faculties and their improvement, must come by exercising the moral powers.

The individual's moral life has social dimensions. When his social relations and social responsibilities are concerned, his moral life involves the happiness of others. From the individual's standpoint, his moral nature can come to fruition only in society; it is

9 *Ibid.*, p. 91.
10 *Millennial Harbinger*, 1836, p. 596.

only in society that it is possible for the individual to reach the highest fulfillment of happiness. Sometimes Campbell connects this portion of his moral philosophy with his view of religion and maintains that "the glory of God is best promoted by achieving the happiness of man." Within society we value certain kinds of life according to the degree to which they promote the happiness of the whole society, or according to their "utility." For instance, certain "callings" or professions are most honored in society because they are most useful to it. From the standpoint of judging any society, that society in which the happiness resulting to mankind is judged highest must have two qualities: 1) it comprehends the greatest variety, and 2) it aims at the largest amount of blessedness to mankind.

Implicit in the foregoing philosophy of morals is a crucial problem concerning Campbell's use of the pleasure-pain principle. In some passages, Campbell's chief interest seems to be the achievement of happiness or pleasure for the individual; in other passages, he is emphatic in making the happiness of others the supreme concern. Like so many other thinkers of his day, Campbell seems to have overlooked the difficulty of reconciling these two aspects of his pleasure-pain principle. For instance, what is man to do when his own personal happiness conflicts with the happiness of mankind? This kind of moral philosophy seems faced with two alternatives: if it clings to the basic assumption that the individual should seek his own pleasure, it would end in a kind of individualistic self-love or egoism; if it emphasizes the sacrifice of the individual's pleasure in the interest of society, it must explain on what principle this should be done. Campbell seems to attempt a combination of love of self with love of others, or enlightened self-love. At least, this appears to be the meaning he gives to the Biblical passage of "love your neighbor as thyself." He interprets this passage as meaning that we are to love our neighbors as much as we do our selves, no more, no less. At the same time, he holds that selfishness is the principle of action which has brought the most evil upon society. How selfishness and altruism are to be managed within the individual's life, how love of self and love of others is to coincide when they are in deep conflict is not clearly worked out in his moral philosophy. There seems to be assumed in his philosophy a view that the pleasures of the individual and the pleasures of society can both be realized in such a manner that neither is sacrificed.

God created the world for His own and man's enjoyment, thus there is a principle of pleasure in the very act of God's creation and in man's purpose on earth. Furthermore, man is put on earth by God who desires man to develop those powers of his own nature which will give him most enjoyment. The supreme pleasure is found in the development of his own character and in achieving the most blessed society. The pleasure-pain principle, adopted by Campbell from the philosophical notions of his day, is harmonized with his notion of the principles of morality found in revealed religion. He believes that the rules or principles which are set forth in the Bible for man's instruction are fashioned upon the "pleasure" principle. [11] When man follows the rules or principles found in the Bible, then his actions will bring happiness to himself and others; when one violates the moral principles in the Bible, he brings suffering to himself and others. If the immorality of the actions is very great, then the suffering may be extended to the next world. Here, again, we see the pleasure-pain principle at work, for this punishment is painful. [12] God created a universe in which physical pain is very hard to bear and in which this pain follows on the breach of the moral laws.

The moral rules and laws to which the pleasure-pain principle is added are "God given," that is, they are revealed in the Bible. But these laws are so constituted that adherence to them will give the greatest amount of pleasure; breaking them will bring the greatest amount of pain. The matter of moral rules or laws having their origin in revealed religion is one of the main points upon which Campbell and Robert Owen disagreed. Campbell does not see how man could originate the moral principles which Owen advocated; these principles had to come from revealed religion. Campbell does not disagree with the view which Owen was putting forth, for love of neighbor is certainly a moral rule, but he chided Owen for not recognizing the *source* of this moral rule.

The harmonizing of the pleasure-pain principle which was so dominant in Enlightenment thinkers with the moral rules and laws in revealed religion is a credit to Campbell's ingenuity. A few years before his death, John Stuart Mill put forth the pleasure-pain principle in a new philosophical dress, but his views were attacked by men of religion as being blasphemy. Mill replied to his religious critics in much the same vein as Campbell had already developed his view of the problem. Mill could not understand a God which would want his creatures to be miserable, unhappy; and he thought that all the martyrs of the church had gone to their deaths because they thought by doing so that the world would be a happier place in which to live. There is little doubt that Alexander Campbell accepted the view of God creating the world for human enjoyment

11 *The Christian System,* p. 31.
12 *Popular Lectures and Addresses;* see essay on "Life and Death," pp. 403-452.

and that the moral laws of the Bible bring the greatest happiness to mankind.

Alexander Campbell's social philosophy, while not a very extensive one, arises out of three conditions of his life and thought. In the first place, he shared many of the attitudes of the Enlightenment thinkers on the "minimal" role of government in the personal and social affairs of men. In the second place, Campbell's thought reflects portions of that philosophy adhered to by so many Christian leaders, particularly Protestants who follow Augustine, that government belongs to the lower part of man's nature or to the "City of man" which cannot be the main concern of those who are dedicated to Christ and His Kingdom. The assumption of the Enlightenment thinkers that the government should stay out of the personal lives of the citizens and the Christian attitude that the members of the Kingdom should stay out of governmental affairs are complementary to one another. [13] But there is another aspect of the historical situation which affected Campbell and others who shared this description of the role of the individual in government and the responsibility of government to the individual. Persons who adopted this philosophy either on philosophical or Christian grounds found themselves caught in the vast social changes of their times, and circumstances forced them to take positions. As a result of these "stay out" and "leave alone" philosophies, a kind of opportunism and doctrine of expediency arose. This being the case, there is little wonder that Campbell's social philosophy reflects vacillating thoughts and positions on some of the major issues he was forced to face. At one time Campbell expounds his philosophy of the Enlightenment social doctrines and Christian withdrawal; at another he takes specific positions which lacked some sort of consistent philosophical basis.

Campbell's admiration for those philosophers who maintained that the government should stay out of the personal and social life of the individual reflects his devotion to the general philosophy of the Enlightenment. On the whole, this was a philosophy of "laissez-faire." At one extreme of this position on the role of government are the anarchists, who desired that all social decisions be left to individuals who can be trusted, they thought, to be moral in their social relations. The anarchists are really extreme laissez-faire philosophers, for they wanted no government at all. Campbell showed some admiration for such a position. Other men did not go so far as the anarchists in demanding no government at all. A philosopher like Locke, for instance, conceded the need for government because of certain inconveniences arising in man's social life. But aside

13 *Millennial Harbinger,* 1845, p. 108.

from military and legal functions along with certain necessary administrative needs, the role of government is quite minimal.

From the standpoint of revealed religion, Campbell's position on governmental and political matters complements the laissez-faire philosophy of certain Enlightenment thinkers. On the religious side, what is uppermost is the individual's devotion to the Kingdom. Ideally, the Christian is not to take part in politics at all, for concern with the selfish pursuits of men which Campbell took politics to be is a lowering of the vision of the Christian life. [14] It is from this kind of reasoning that he attacks "patriotism" as a kind of collective selfishness. [15] The Christian works for the reconstruction of life not through governmental action, but through the church and through individual moral and religious action. When governments are viewed under the aspect of eternity, it is seen that governments come and go, are changing and transient, but the Christian system stretches from the First Cause to the Last End of all things. Furthermore, there is no New Testament version of what form any government should be, although Campbell's version of the millennial idea shows preferences for a ceratin kind of democracy.

If the New Testament supports no particular form of government, how does democracy as a form of government arise? Campbell finds the origins of democracy on grounds other than revealed religion, which is a somewhat different position from that of the American Puritans who found the origin of democracy in the Old Testament in such passages which contained phrases like "choose ye leaders." While Campbell never treated the problem of the origin of democracy in detail, there is one statement in his resolution which he presented to the Virginia State Convention which reads: "Whereas republican institutions and the blessings of Government originated in, and must always depend upon, the intelligence, virtue and patriotism of the community . . . ." Here we see that he attributes the origin of democracy to a natural outgrowth of associated living.

Campbell's philosophy of history is primarily optimistic, as were so many others in the age in which he lived. This is not to say that he was not aware of the personal and social evils which prevailed; but the cure for all these evils was to be effected by one simple remedy. The restoration of the New Testament church, a return to the program of the Christian dispensation, would bring peace and happiness upon the earth. This would come about when "genuine Christianity" is diffused through all nations. It is only then that wars, crimes, punishments will cease. Governments "will rest upon

14 *Ibid.*, 1833, p. 12.
15 *Ibid.*, 1832, pp. 114-116.

just and benevolent principles." This is Campbell's view of the Golden Age of mankind; it is a view which holds that the Golden Age in the future is assured by returning to the principles of the past. His picture of such a world is thus: "The seasons will become more mild; the climates more salubrious, health more vigorous, labor less, lands more fertile, and the animal creation more prolific; for the knowledge of the glory of God shall cover the whole earth as the waters cover the channels of the sea." [16]

On the issue of the relation of the church to the state, Campbell brought with him from the old country several strong separatist convictions. The historical background of the long fight to rid the British islands of the domination by the Roman Catholic church, and the further fight of separating the church from the domination of any government, had figured in his experience. There was also the more recent struggle in Ireland over the support of the nationally established church by Presbyterians who had their own church but by law were required to support the church of England. Some reformers wanted the "purification" of the church to go as far as to completely separate church and state. Another element in Campbell's views on the relation of church and state stemmed from the Enlightenment thinkers who, as has been shown, thought government should have as little to say about the lives of its citizens as possible. The third element was the Christian desire to be "above" politics. All of these influences led Campbell to attack the Catholic church and to maintain that organized religion and political power should be widely separated.

Campbell's social philosophy is an excellent example of one which supports certain principles of "stay out" and "leave alone" for the role of government, yet is forced to take positions involving social and political matters when it comes to grips with pressing social problems. During his time in America, Campbell was caught in the slavery issue. While he searched hard to find Biblical principles to guide him on the issue, he obtained little Biblical help on the problem.[17] Campbell finally emerged as neither pro-slavery nor abolitionist, even though both of these positions can cite and did cite Biblical support for their positons. On such social matters as war and capital punishment, both of which Campbell opposed, he did some Biblical searching, but his views emerge more as an outcome of his philosophy of the Enlightenment than of Biblical pronouncements.

Campbell thinks that the moral culture should be united with the intellectual culture, not merely in the private instruction in the

[16] *Ibid.*, 1841, p. 9.
[17] Harold L. Lunger, *The Political Ethics of Alexander Campbell* (St. Louis: The Bethany Press, 1954).

home, the public schools, the church, but in a college curriculum. This viewpoint, along with other reasons, led him into a philosophy of education.

Even a Newton, says Campbell, entered life "without a single idea," and he adds, "so have all the men of all ages of time." [18] Campbell carries this basic assumption over into his educational philosophy and he analyzes the learning process as originating in the child's first impressions. He writes: "The first impression is that of pain — the first action, complaint. Thus man in making his debut on the theatre of life, enters with a shriek. The child of agony, he agonizes on his first recontre with the very elements of his existence. He feels before he thinks, and therefore his mind itself is stimulated to action. Thus, man begins to learn." [19] From this insight we learn that it is from the stimulation of the sensory organs that man is prodded into learning. Out of these stimulations, feelings arise; and out of feelings man's intellectual powers are brought into play. Campbell is direct and clear on the origin of the learning process: "But how does he learn? First, undoubtedly, by sensation, then by reflection."

This empirical approach to education places the newly born child in the "school of nature;" a condition which God created so that "the first impression of the attributes of things upon the new born infant compelled it to begin to learn." Campbell then shows that the wisdom of God in contriving such a human situation for learning had not been accurately observed or followed, but if it had been "undeviatingly practiced upon ages before Bacon was born, the world would have been ages in advance of what it is now." Campbell claims that he learned this philosophy of education from nature itself. When man is placed upon the earth in this natural environment, it is Mother Nature that first arrests the attention of her students. One of the most primitive ways that Mother Nature does this to her pupil is "by salting him with oxygen as soon as he enters her portico." Man in nature is aroused to action by making it to his "interest" and his "happiness" to learn.

If all ideas come from sensation and reflection, then the sensory experiences of a human being from earliest childhood are extremely important. This means that the sounds, colors, sizes, shapes, and tastes of objects as they confront the child are the starting places of learning. In Campbell's empirical method, the eyes and the ears are regarded, as by many thinkers, the most important of all the sense organs as the means by which sensations enter the human mind. He writes: "Among purely general branches of education

18 *Millennial Harbinger*, 1835, p. 152 f.
19 *Ibid.*, p. 152.

there are, however, two, which in our country have not yet gained the position which they deserve. I speak of the training of the eye and the ear, the noblest of the special faculties by which external phenomena enter the mind." [20] Campbell thinks that the ear had been given preference in much of educational experience, but with the development of the physical sciences, the use of the eye would come into greater prominence.

The various programs which Campbell worked out as practical proposals for education followed from this premise concerning the importance of the sensory organs in gaining knowledge. In the program of Bethany College, one year each of psychology, botany, chemistry, astronomy, geology, and zoology were required. In one of the programs proposed for the public schools he includes the sciences of geography, of "material and animated nature," and "self-knowledge." In regard to the public school curriculum, he thinks that sciences like chemistry would be helpful in teaching students how to make the soil fertile. He thinks that Nature, as the first teacher of things scientific, should be made, therefore, the subject-matter of formal study in common schools and colleges alike.

Campbell's view of the importance of early childhood means that the child must be instructed, must have his life directed by examples, and must be trained. This makes the role that parents and teachers play in a child's educational experience very important and essential to his formation. In fact, it is here that the real reformation must take place — in early education. He says: "If anyone would reform and bless mankind, let him give them good and intelligent parents and school-masters, and less than a tithe of all other reformers." [21] The importance of early education led Campbell to be a pioneer in the cause of the education of women. As mothers spend most time with small children, their influence is greatest and should be guided by a high degree of education. The child needs the mother's aid in its training. Of all the techniques for teaching — instruction, examples, training — it is training that is more important; for instructon and examples often fail. Campbell is emphatic on this point: "Very many have good precepts and good examples before them, but because of lack of training, are neither an ornament nor a blessing to society." [22]

Any philosophy of education that is not foreign to human nature must take account of man's capacities, what his mind can do and cannot do. Campbell adopts a psychology of man which held that, in some respects, man's mind is passive — it receives the sensations

20 Ibid., p. 152.
21 Ibid., 1841, p. 480.
22 Ibid., 1841, p. 480.

which nature forces upon it. In other respects, man's mind is active, in the functions of perception, composition, discrimination, abstraction, imagination, and retention. With this analysis of mental activities, it is clear that Campbell holds to a "faculty" psychology, a view which maintains that the training of one faculty of the mind has no bearing upon the other faculties. Man's mind is divided into separate functions, each distinct and unaffected by the others. For instance, Campbell does not think that the training of the imagination would give one a good memory. The memory, the imagination, the powers of perception, the powers of abstraction must all be trained, but each must be trained separately.

Campbell believes in the education of the entire personality of man, but how are the seemingly unrelated parts of man's nature to be bound together? How are the various disciplines of man's educational experience to be brought together and made to function in an organized whole? In other words, Campbell has a problem of "integration" when he starts with a faculty psychology. He never really considers this problem in a detailed analysis; he does, however, want integration, and he seeks to organize all of man's intellectual endeavors under the eternal aspects of religion and morality. Literature, science, and art all come under this domain. As young minds come to understand the universe in which they are living and inquiring into, they should realize that the design, utility, and beauty of everything can be traced to an eternal source. This means that everything that is learned is related to the perfections and designs of God. Even the archetypes of the universe, those ideas of man which form the highest reaches of knowledge, must be seen as originating in the infinite and eternal intelligence of the Creator. This thought is closer to Leibniz than to Locke, and it makes for an intimate relation between the mind of God and the eternal forms of the universe. Thus, the study of the universe with its beauty, melody, and harmony in nature and society, must engage the affections, the admiration, and the love of every inquirer for Him who created the universe and all that is in it. Campbell thought that if knowledge of the universe is presented in this way, then young minds will come under the divine influence and will secure their hearts to all that is good, and honorable, and excellent in heaven and earth. In this manner he thought that man could achieve an integrated life, one that is full of harmony and unity. The dualisms and splits which issue from a faculty psychology of man could be overcome by the heart following where the mind leads it, and the harmony of mind and heart would bring that integration into man's life without which life is fragmented and divided.

One of the most significant aspects of Alexander Campbell's philosophy of education is found in his proposals and practices concerning the use of the Bible in the schools, both private and public. [23] As we know from his views of the Bible in general, the only means by which mankind can learn religious and moral facts is from the revealed truth contained in the Scriptures. It will be recalled that all religious and moral principles of non-Christian religions had their source in Biblical literature. It will be recalled, too, that Campbell advocates that the Bible be read according to the linguistic principles used in the sudy of any other ancient document. His methods also require a knowledge of Hebrew, Greek, and other languages, such as Latin. But the empirical method as Campbell conceives it and the application of this method to the Scriptures was not in existence to any large extent during his day in America, thus he started an attack upon the leading seminaries and private schools with religious programs.

The attack Campbell made upon the theological schools cannot be understood unless one recalls that he made certain assumptions about the source of religious beliefs and the kind of scholarship which he deems necessary to obtain these beliefs. If theological schools in his day were teaching the creeds and beliefs which had grown up since the New Testament times, then, of course, they were open to criticism on his grounds. He holds that such schools were perpetuating the grounds for division which had split the church for over eighteen hundred years. His attack was not only upon the Catholic church, but upon many Protestant groups as well. In fact, he criticizes any group which did not seek to restore primitive Christianity and had replaced it wth extra-Biblical ideas and theologies.

What Campbell finds wrong with theological education in his day thus stems from his view of the role of the Bible in man's knowledge of God and of moral principles generally. The basic proposition to be understood in Campbell's position is that the Bible is a *non-sectarian* book. [24] As such, there is no place for a Presbyterian, a Baptist, or a Catholic Bible. There is only one truth — the truth contained in Biblical literature. There is only one Lord, one faith, one baptism. What had happened in theological schools which Campbell was attacking was that these schools did not regard the Bible as a non-sectarian book, as a book of literature, as a book to be studied in the manner in which all good scholarship must proceed. The schools were using the Bible and the creeds to divide the church and to sustain themselves with a professional clergy. His outburst against them was damaging and certain of his passages on the subject would make it seem as if he was advocating that these

23 *Popular Lectures and Addresses,* p. 244.
24 *Ibid.,* p. 244.

schools should be done away with, but this was not the case. Their method of study was wrong, and their intention was wrong, but not their interest in things religious or their devotion to Biblical literature as sacred. Their failings were that they were unscholarly and unscientific.

When Campbell develops his own positive views of the place of the Bible in both religious and public schools, the idea of the canon as a non-sectarian book pervades his whole argument. First, the place of the Bible in higher education is seen in the program he started at Bethany College. The purpose of higher education in Campbell's educational philosophy is that colleges and seminaries have the responsibility of training the teachers and ministers that communities need. The curriculum at Bethany included lectures each day on Sacred history. But on Campbell's views there is nothing denominational about Sacred history; it is the only record man had of religious ideas, and it is the only way in which a person can enlighten himself on matters of this kind. Other schools had for many generations made the Bible a subject-matter for study; this procedure was as old as the first schools among the colonists. But Campbell's adoption of the Bible as a text-book has this difference; the Bible is regarded as literature to be studied by scholarly techniques and without denominational bias.

When Campbell advocates that the Bible be put into the common schools, it is not to foster any sect or religious denomination. He sees no inconsistency of having the Bible taught in the common schools with his clear and strong beliefs about the separation of church and state. To teach the Bible in a critical and scholarly way is not to advocate any church relationship to the state. The church organizaion is to be entirely free and separate from governmental control, thus the problem is stated as two separate issues in his mind — one is the Bible as the source of all religious and moral ideas in his theory of knowledge and the other is the matter of voluntary and private congregations as opposed to a state church.

Campbell does think that there would be some consequences of the adoption of the Bible as a subject of study in private and common schools. He thinks that the free and critical study of the Bible would cut the ground from under the Catholic church. When man can read for himself what the Scriptures say, when he has learned to read with a critical mind and with the best linguistic tools at his command, then no authoritarian religous body can enslave his intelligence or the operation of his free mind.

In the resolution on public schools which Campbell prepared for the Virginia state convention, he holds that education is essential to a democracy. His main contention is that "neither intelligence nor virtue can be maintained or promoted in any community without education." After establishing that education is a proper interest and function of government, Campbell then proceeds to show us why he thinks education in a community so important. Two aspects of the community culture are involved in his beliefs: the moral virtues in one area and the intellectual development in the other. Since it is the business of government to prevent crime and to create those conditions which are conducive to the making of good citizens, the main avenue through which this can be accomplished is public education. Ignorance is connected with idleness and idleness is connected with immorality and crime in every degree. On the intellectual side of man's developmnt, government has another duty. The basic proposition from which Campbell's argument proceeds is that "universal suffrage requires universal education." Campbell could not see how a commonwealth could have a very effective democracy without enlightened citizens. In one of his most fervent addresses he pleaded for schools to educate the people who could not read or write in the western part of Virginia. Although these people were illiterate, they had the right to vote, and Campbell thought that this was one of the most serious conditions in the state at the time. Without education and development of the intellectual powers, man is more like an animal, and it is the proper function of the state to maintain schools which would remove ignorance and promote intelligence and virtue. Campbell then concludes that it is the purpose of education "to promote the public good."

Many of Campbell's practical proposals in education are quite modern when viewed against the time and circumstance of American history. He wanted the common schools to be free to all children, tax-supported by the entire community, and he desired that the teachers be competent. The teachers could be trained in an institution of higher learning or they could be self-educated, and if the latter, he advocated examinations so that they could be certified. Furthermore, the schools for the community should be conveniently located so that all children could have access to them.

Campbell's educational philosophy is an outgrowth of his general philosophy of empiricism and his religious commitment to revealed religion. His view that man's mind is molded by his sensory experiences which it gathers into itself, makes early training, instruction, and example important. This empirical philosophy also has implications concerning what man learns from nature and from the experience of others. It leads Campbell to make the sciences a significant part of the school and college curricula, and it leads him to emphasize practical sciences for the average man.

But man does not live by exercise of his intellectual powers alone. Man is a moral being, and some provision must be made for the union of intellectual and moral culture. Moral education is doubly important, for the moral powers of man are more difficult to develop. The source of moral principles is the Bible, and the Bible must be an important part of a common school and college curricula. Campbell could not see how the proper function of government, the function of promoting the general welfare, could be accomplished without enlightened citizens. And these citizens should be intellectually competent and morally responsible.

VI

THE LEGACY OF ALEXANDER CAMPBELL

Many of the themes with which Alexander Campbell wrestled are perennial, stretching across the centuries of man's philosophic and religious quest; other of his themes are parochial in time, momentary in significance, sometimes trivial. The perennial themes are those of the relation of faith to reason, of revelation to natural happenings, of symbols and meanings to reality, of science to morals. And there have always been the perplexing problems of man's relation to God, to nature, and to his fellow man. The estimate of Campbell as a thinker on these deep and penetrating problems of human existence is elevated when the main contentions he put forth are selected and sifted out of his multitudinous writings and shown to have depth and range of meaning.

Alexander Campbell belongs to a time-segment of the Christian movement. It is a segment which was influenced by the philosophy of the Renaissance, the Enlightenment, and the Scottish Common Sense school, as well as by Utilitarianism; by the religious thought of the broader aspects of the Protestant movement, of the specialized Puritan and Restoration goals and the Dutch Covenant theological elements within that movement. He sought to weld these philosophical and religious trends together into a new synthesis, a synthesis which borrowed and rejected something from each, and which would result in an outlook and a program of life which was intellectually and emotionally satisfying.

There is little wonder that the more traditional elements of the Christian movement opposed Campbell and many of the beliefs for which he stood. In many ways he was a threat to their institutional and intellectual security. At the same time, he was not an intellectual and institutional radical such as Thomas Paine or Robert Owen, both of whom he criticized for sharing thoughts and proposing institutional innovations contrary to human experience as he conceived it. The cautious and conservative are afraid of intellectual and social innovations; the experimental and radical are distrustful of tradition. Campbell was cautious and conservative in some respects, experimental and radical in others. He was traditional and conservative in holding fast to the commemorative institutions of Christianity, Baptism and the Lord's Supper which dated from Biblical days; he was traditional and conservative in his respect for the Bible as the Revealed Word of God and in his views that revelation had a special meaning through the centuries. He was experimental and radical in discounting the creeds, in rejecting as central certain dogmas which had entered the lore of the Christian faith, and in his refusal to sanction certain institutional practices and rituals which had grown up in the long history of the Christian movement. In a world grown complex and weary with a superstructure of belief and practice, he sought a principle, the principle of restoration, to winnow out what was primary and essential to the Christian life.

Christianity has often opposed novel ideas and practices only to find itself later absorbing them. By the time Alexander Campbell appeared on the historical scene, the Christian movement was already in the process of accepting scientific methods and conclusions, of proclaiming the insights of the Renaissance concerning man's dignity and reliance on his own initiative and creativity, and of absorbing the Enlightenment emphasis upon the importance of sensory facts and observations. By Campbell's time the Protestant revolt had become an intellectual and institutional movement with its own principles and its own conscious destiny. This is not to say that there were not diverse and contradictory elements within the Protestant movement generating a variety of intellectual and practical innovations, for these can be seen as partaking of the individualistic principles underlying Protestantism as a whole. This is why the immediate movements preceding and contemporary with Campbell's life, the movements of Puritanism and the Restoration movement, in particular, can be explained in terms of Protestant principles and their consequences. There is the further fact that the philosophic notion of nominalism or individualism only buttressed the Protestant notion of religious individualism, and at the same time led to diversities and sometimes to absurdities in social practice.

It is a truism that the live options of one age become the dead ones of another. Thus, even the perennial problem of the relation of faith to reason assumes a meaning and a statement in one age, and often to one generation, which is not the same or is expressed in the same way for another. One of Campbell's particular views of faith, namely, faith as mental assent to a factual statement and a belief in another's testimony is common to his intellectual age and climate, and while this view of faith has its merits in certain contexts, subsequent experience has driven the matter of faith into more subjective intentions. Campbell's view of reason, while partly meritorous in emphasizing the gathering of facts, overlooks the value of hypothetical thinking and at times flatly rejects it. In other words, subsequent philosophical and religious thinking has made faith narrower and reason broader in their meanings than Campbell conceived them.

Furthermore, religious thinkers in the century since Campbell's passing have come to distrust the reason which Campbell adored. The contemporary revolt against reason in religious matters has made more poignant the reality of faith. The paradoxes of reason have been pointed up and have been used to show the inadequacy of reason as a justification of faith. Part of the contemporary revolt against reason, at least against a narrow conception of reason, no doubt stems from the experience of generations subsequent to Campbell who have seen how reason can be used by evil men to calculate and deliberately plan for total destruction and annihilation. They have seen how facts, even Biblical facts, can be selected, arranged, and quoted to support evil purposes. The distrust of reason, the extreme subjectivity of faith, and the new emphasis upon the demonic in human nature are qualities which mark a different mood of the times from that of Campbell's, an age which has not yet found a proper place for reason in its religious experience.

Generations of subsequent religious thinkers undoubtedly would think that Campbell restricted revelation too much. Perhaps there would be no quarrel in general with Campbell's acceptance of the Bible as the Revealed Word of God, but even here there would be some disagreement over the meanings of these terms. Such later day theologians as Paul Tillich and Richard Niebuhr see revelation in a different light. While most contemporary religious thinkers would agree that there are levels of experiential quality and religious worth appearing at different times within Biblical history, the Covenant theology which affords the basis for Campbell's distinctions of the various levels of worth in the Bible is relegated to a near-forgotten segment of the Christian movement.

There is always the perplexing problem of the relation of symbols to experience, of how symbols represent experience and of how they re-direct and control it. It is the merit of a symbol that it is non-temporal, that it cuts across centuries of recorded experience. A symbol can be recorded easily, remembered in thought, and recalled with ease. Furthermore, symbols have different uses in man's expression, and as Campbell noted, some symbols enter into a context of allegory, some assume poetic forms, and some operate as factual statements. Campbell was far ahead of many of his age in holding that the purposes for which symbolic formulations are used are important, a necessary analysis in explicating the meanings of the Scritptures. Thus, Campbell was not a "literalist," or one who reduces all forms of symbolic expression to the factual one. On the other hand, Campbell did not develop a systematic theory of the role of metaphor and myth in Christian writings and their place in leading to and directing religious experience.

A symbol can have similar spelling throughout its history in a given language, and it can be translated from one language to another as Hebrew, Greek, Aramaic, and Latin texts have become available in English. Campbell was aware of many of the powers and functions of symbols, but he failed to develop a theory of how symbols take on an accumulation of meanings and how symbols change in their meaings, of what they denote and what they imply. Symbols like "God," "Messiah," "faith," "revelation," do not remain absolutely fixed in their meanings; they move in history as well as through history. However, symbols must retain some core of their meanings if they are to have any continuity with their past, and it is to Campbell's credit that he sought to establish as carefully as he could the original meanings of the Biblical texts. His attempt to "restore" the original meanings of the Bible was part of his effort to establish a basis for agreement and unity among all Christians. So zealous was Campbell about determining the exact Biblical meaning of a word or group of words that he almost, but not quite, equated the words of the Bible with the Word of God.

Alexander Campbell saw no threat to religious values in the advance of science, in its methods or results. In the spirit of Francis Bacon and of Isaac Newton he held that the more one learned of the universe, the more he could understand the creativity of God. God made the world out of His own compassion, and he fashioned it upon a moral basis, that is, certain acts lead to consequences which are certain death or pain, while other acts lead to consequences which are fulfilling and pleasurable. The pleasure-pain principle underwrites all of man's experience, intellectual as well as moral, but in the final end the moral life and the "noble man" is the goal of all creation. While it is true that Campbell expresses the mood of his times in believing that individual acts of goodness lead to a composite good and social harmony, a principle very close to Adam Smith's economic and moral theories, it is equally true that he never developed a sense of the tragic in human existence. Evil there was as a fact, but it was an evil to be overcome and conquered; it was not an evil to live with and to come to terms with and to endure. Campbell's moral optimism belongs to an age which had not taken into itself the agonies of suffering and of living with a painful conscience.

Campbell's love of nature and his love of God were so simple and straight-forward that he never felt estranged from either. Given his assumptions about man's relation to God and man's relation to the nature which God created, it would be difficult for him to feel the loneliness, estrangement, and alienation which marks the contemporary mood. The problems and concerns of men have shifted since Campbell's time, and man's relation to God, takes on a different meaning, a meaning which looks upon men like Campbell as child-like in their approach to God. Campbell's faith in God proceeded from his belief in God's love enveloping nature and each individual man, and his trust in God was not something which grew out of the agony and despair of feeling alone and alienated.

It was remarked earlier that Campbell considered some problems which were momentary, insignificant, and trivial. Some of these notions passed fleetingly from his thought; even so, some of his pronouncements developed into major contentions for his followers, grounds for further divisions within the Christian movement. As such, these views, some of which he outgrew, became ghostly consequences of his over-stated conclusions. A few of these should be mentioned, since they make up a bulk of literature in books, articles, and pamphlets which deal with issues of division which are travesties on a great man's life and thought. Most of these divisions among Campbell's followers have been made not upon the so called doctrinal "beliefs" which he held, but upon the "practices" which he advocated. For instance, at an early stage of his thinking, Campbell thought that the function of the church proper was being overshadowed, if not completely obscured, and sometimes even replaced, by organizations which had grown up along side it. Later, he changed his mind on some of these organizations and became an advocate, even an officer, in a few of them. But his followers never forgot his early admonitions, and they continued the debates over the acceptance or non-acceptance of missionary societies, schools and seminaries. As the organizational life of the group developed over the past one hundred years, this cleavage deepened on matters of "organized" work done cooperatively by the churches. The so-called "higher boards" of missionary work, colleges, pension funds, benevolence, state and national organizations brought forth a violent reaction from those who retained an "independent" approach. "Cooperative" work and "independent" work became a central issue for many of Campbell's followers.

There is little doubt that the cleavage which developed within the group which Campbell formed stems from a misunderstanding of his view of philosophical nominalism, to use a technical term, that is, of the meaning of "independence" and "individualism," and his view of the collective life and functions. While Campbell did emphasize the role of the individual in all phases of the life of man and nature, it has been noted repeatedly in the foregoing chapters that he thought that no individual stands alone in the universe. This notion applies to atoms in a natural order, to single bones in our bodies, to man in society, and to the individual church in the Christian system. It is part of Campbell's philosophy and religion that the feelings, functions, and integrity of the individual in any part of God's creation must be respected, appreciated, and loved; it is equally true, however, that an individual unit standing alone and isolated has no meaning, function, or purpose. To find its own meaning and destiny it must relate itself to an orderly and organized whole, natural, social, or religious. Thus, the "lost" individual in Campbell's system of thought is an unrelated, isolated, and completely segregated unit, lacking in meaning and purpose. When this condition occurs, it is proper to speak of a "lost" individual church as well as a "lost" individual man.

Campbell's attempt to establish the two "commemorative" institutions of the Christian life, Baptism and the Lord's Supper, also created grounds for divisions among his followers. Campbell thought the original meaning of the term "Baptism" signified "immersion," and his restoration principle demanded a return to this primitive form. But soon there came the problem of transfers of memberships from other church groups which had used a different form of Baptism. Some followers of Campbell re-defined Baptism in various ways, one being immersion in Christ's spirit and accepted people who came to them, even though these persons were unimmersed in water. This practice became known as "open membership," and if it did not create new organizational divisions, it deepened many of the cleavages already there. On the matter of the Lord's Supper, or the observance of the commemoration of Christ, the main point Campbell had made regarding the particular form was that it should be done decently and in good order. But there soon arose specific questions about the use of one cup from which all participants drank or cups designed for each individual. At first, the problem was one of restoration to and deviation from the practice of the primitive New Testament church, but later the issue of hygiene entered into the debate. A further controversy arose over the nature of the wine, whether fermented or non-fermented; and of the loaf, broken or unbroken. And these are not the only points of controversy over the specific practices of both Baptism and the Lord's Supper; there seemed to be no end to new angles of contention and division.

The nature of church organization posed further problems and led to more divisions. Campbell unconsciously adopted the "democratic" climate of his day in organizational life and applied it to the church. It is true that he sought a definite "prescription" for the organizational structure of the church based upon primitive New Testament times, and it is now obvious that he ignored some of the early organizational structures and selected those he favored. The "congregational" structure of organization, with its "Elders" and "Deacons" became the settled one. But more important from the standpoint of later divisions was the matter of the use of "instruments" in the church. The pulpit or lectern was placed in the center of the church to signify that "preaching" was of central importance. On the pulpit was placed a Bible to indicate that it, too, was central. Usually the baptistry and the Lord's Table occupied the center of the building. Thus, the baptistry, the pulpit, the Bible, and the Lord's Table, all occupied the center of attention and of importance. Much of this philosophy of the place and use of these instruments is shared by other congregationally structured churches. But the real issue of Campbell's followers arose over the use of instruments for music. Musical inventions, such as the organ and the piano, had entered on the cultural scene in post-Biblical times, and a group of people dedicated to the "radical restoration" of the primitive church would have none of these. At best, a tuning fork might be admitted into the worship program, but even this modern invention was rejected by some. The aesthetic nature of worship, the newer aids to a religious experience, the creation of a dignified and holy atmosphere were sacrificed by some in adherence to an unrelenting principle. Sometimes the issue of the use or non-use of instrumental music reached a point of absurdity, as somewhere I have read of a congregation which denied a person the privilege of singing in its choir because that person had false teeth, and this was, in fact, using instrumental music.

The consequences of a man's thought and life may take many devious and ironic turns, as the foregoing sketch shows. There is always the trivial and the absurd, the momentary and the fleeting, which make up a part of the consequences of any thought-system or any prescription for action. But the insignificant and absurd, the derived and secondary, ought not to overshadow the primary and central dedication of a man's whole life and teaching. A re-evaluation of Alexander Campbell's ultimate commitment helps to put his life's work and thought in proper perspective. The disunity of Christendom challenged his fertile mind and was always on his agonizing conscience. The search for a principle of unity, intellectually respectable and morally acceptable, was the driving power of his life. This principle of unity has broad outlines, outlines into which could be fit the trivial and absurd if one wishes, but it is a principle which on the whole has intellectual integrity and moral respectability. This was and is Alexander Campbell's legacy, but it is a legacy which must be put in proper perspective by considering what has taken place historically and is taking place currently in church life in order to see the fullness of its meaning and appeal.

The Protestant revolution had set forth in the world new

psychological energies which broke the bounds of the old institutional restrictions. Political toleration and indifference (and sometimes political support for some groups) made for a social climate which promoted division after division. Not the least among the strong factors nurturing division in religious institutions, of course, was economic opportunity. A new group could support itself economically because political and cultural conditions allowed it. The alliance of church and state in country after country had been able for centuries to control religious innovations and under this condition no new religious organizations could emerge. But political and economic conditions changed, both in fact and in the rational justification of their positions, thus new religious organizations could emerge in a climate which made economic maintenance possible. Political processes and the philosophies which supported them made possible cultural freedom, and cultural freedom meant free association and the chance to organize new groups. Furthermore, the mood of the times fostered individualism, inventiveness, and experimentation. Armed with the principles that every man is a priest, the authority of individual conscience, the accountability of the individual only to God, and the natural rights theory, strong and powerful individuals arose to lead whole throngs of people, to arouse their impulses into loyalty and sometimes fanatic devotion. The romantic interpretation of religious history undoubtedly overemphasizes the role of the "great man," but there is a sense in which this interpretation is partially correct. For great religious leaders have had strong personal appeal and as founders of vast religious movements they evoked responses of undying devotion from their followers.

The age of individualism in economic life produced its empire builders, and in many ways this empire building impulse invaded religious movements. A strong and dominating personality in religion could sway the emotions of large numbers of people, walk out of an established church taking hundreds, even thousands, of people with him. Cultural conditions made it possible for him to sustain himself economically and socially in his new venture. A part of the colorful, if not so admirable, history of the period to which Alexander Campbell belonged is that a strong and powerful leader could persuade a whole congregation to follow his "voice crying in the wilderness" for some significant or trivial reform of Christian belief and practice.

But this individualism in religious movements, creative in some respects, had also its sordid effects. Strong and powerful men are often jealous of other strong and powerful men. Their envy and pride results in vicious attacks upon their competitors for the souls of men. They often harangue their followers to be loyal, to disregard the appeals of their competitors. They assassinate each other's characters, participate in unholy name-calling, and make anti-Christs of their personal enemies. These practices, of course, bring more divisions or deepen the cleavages which are already there. As the mood of the times changes and the dignity of the competition is elevated, these bad practices fade from the religious scene. Today if a minister should behave in this way it would be considered bad taste.

Alexander Campbell ignored the social, economic, and political grounds for the divisions which had occurred in Christendom. He tended to analyze the causes of division on the grounds of intellectual errors and scholarly deficiencies. He did think that many groups perpetuated themselves through seminaries which kept alive their preferred creeds, but this was due to ignorance rather than to other causes. Men simply do not "think right," do not formulate their beliefs in philosophy and religion on adequate scholarly and intellectual grounds. Thus, he steadfastly sought to bring the minds of his contemporaries to some intellectual basis for the union of all Christians. He sought to cut the grounds from under their foundations of faith and practice and to demonstrate the Biblical way to unity.

The growth of the corporate society in America was just getting under way when Campbell passed from the scene. His message had been addressed to rural America, to an agricultural society whose independence and self-reliance had grown partly, at least, out of their pioneering experiences. His appeal to the individual believer matched the independent impulses already there. Self-reliance and self-sufficiency of the individual are qualities which demand a robust religious appeal. It is interesting to note that the transferred theologies from the old country, Puritanism in New England for instance, which first emphasized the helplessness of man gave way to a more robust faith when the situation changed.

In the hundred years since Campbell's passing, however, America has grown into a corporate society. Large corporations, large schools, large churches became more and more the pattern of culture. At present, new trends are developing in these corporate groups, in business, education, and religion, the most significant of these being that of mergers. The basic value involved in these corporate mergers, whether economic or religious, appears to be that of "efficiency," and the desire to eliminate overlapping functions. It is interesting to note that the arguments given for church mergers often parallel those given for organizational mergers in the business world, if one looks below the surface.

There seems to be another factor operating in the present movement toward mergers in church life. One of the most powerful forces creating a certain kind of unity, a force which undoubtedly played a part in the unity of the early Christians, is the fear of a deadly enemy. In many countries of the contemporary world, especially where some kind of Marxism has flourished, the church has been on the defensive. In country after country the activities of the church have been curtailed, their functions limited primarily to the performance of ceremony. Faced with the prospects of increasing curtailment of powers and functions, there is little wonder that Roman Catholics (who have had the most to lose in the struggle with the Marxists) and some Protestants are wooing each other in the interest of a united front. Faced with a threat of curtailment, even annihilation in some cases, it is not surprising that various groups which have heretofore been enemies now look for common ties of tradition as a basis for union. Some Protestant groups are proclaiming that they find more in common with Roman Catholics than they thought they had. At the same time, Roman Catholics are making modifications in doctrine, in ceremony, in clerical dress, and in the democratization of their organizational life, and there is every indication that all these changes are more compatible with Protestant tradition and feeling.

The foregoing analysis shows "causes" for mergers and unions, not "reasons" for them. There is a different kind of unity of Christendom which is more positive, more creative, and more enduring. The unity created by economic efficiency is hardly a respectable value system for ultimate survival; the unity of self-defense in the presence of a deadly enemy is at best of temporary worth; the unity of traditional bonds is backward looking and hardly strong enough to face a challenging future. The kind of unity which Alexander Campbell envisioned for Christendom is conceptual and practical, and this kind of unity is based upon internal qualities, qualities which give the movement a positive outlook, a creative impulse, and an enduring force. Qualities generated in a movement out of desire for efficiency, out of fear of a deadly enemy, out of the bonds of tradition are too often externally imposed and give little creative commitment or meaning to existence.

On the conceptual or ideational side of his plea for unity, Alexander Campbell made the requirement for discipleship all important. He admitted that what he advocated was a simplicity of faith, which cut away the superstructure of a vast number of irrelevant beliefs. Commitment to Christ is the basic requirement. Of course, this phrase is fused with a multitude of meanings, meanings which have expanded and deepened with religious experience, but that is as it should be. To many, no doubt, the simple demand is too vague, allows too much to enter into the conceptual and even the organizational boundaries of the Christian movement. It is true that the definitional boundary of the term at times has narrowed and at other times expanded as it moves through history. Obviously, the definitional boundary of a Christian cannot be expanded to include anything and everything, or as is sometimes argued that all men are religious because they are devoted to somebody or to something or to some goal; on the other hand, the definitional boundary cannot be narrowed to justify the exclusion of a person because of his race or used to justify the persecution of a group such as the Jews. Nevertheless, commitment to Christ seems a proper starting place as a basis for the unity of all Christians and the search for all the relevant meanings of this phrase brings to light those positive and creative qualities which make the Christian movement have uniqueness in its surrounding world. This is Alexander Campbell's great insight into a positive Christian unity.

Campbell selected Baptism and the Lord's Supper as the two most important institutions in the history of Christianity. These became the observances around which men through the centuries tie themselves with the past and through which they can experience a newness of life for facing the future. While it is true that the Christian movement at large, and Campbell's followers in particular, have had many disagreements concerning the proper manner in which these acts are to be performed, there has been little doubt as to their primary importance. It is a sociological fact that any movement must have broad outlines defining the nature of its rituals or the whole experience ends up in chaos. These broad outlines must allow some deviations, else there will be uniformity which becomes a stifling conformity. Campbell's approach to the Lord's Supper offers some interesting suggestions which might heal the divisions which have accumulated around this observance. Primarily, the Lord's Supper is a commemoration of Christ, and it has traditional bonds, but as to the *manner* of its specific practice it is a matter of religious art and beauty. The dignity and good order, regardless of the specific materials used or the manner of partaking, is the main criterion of the choice of the form of the ceremony.

The problem of uniformity and deviation, of rigid habits of ritual order over against flexible ones, is one which Christians need to consider and use to achieve a deeper understanding of the nature of ceremony in general. It should now be a truism that extreme conformity of belief and practice does not allow "commitment to Christ" to expand and deepen; it does not allow the experience of Baptism to take on new and deeper meanings; it does not allow the commemoration of Christ to find new ventures into the many qualities of his rich personality. It must be obvious that some kinds of unity are stifling, choking of individuality. (Witness the kind of unity and conformity attempted both in politics and in religion by the Nazi Germans.) On the other hand, some kinds of unities are flexible enough to allow deviations, to allow the search for the new and novel in emerging, creative experience. And it should be equally obvious that some kinds of divisions are socially, religiously, and morally destructive, while other kinds of divisions are creative and wholesome. Unity without uniformity does not mean chaos, nor does it mean conformity. It means a balance of the broad religious habits of ritual and the habits of creativity which is in good aesthetic taste.

The foregoing interpretation of the habits of ritual and ceremony may seem to some people a kind of weasel suggestion, vacillating between rigidity one moment and flexibility another. Such ambivalent responses are not intended. In the first place, the basis which Campbell advocated for Christian union is not lost. It becomes a working formula for the broad outlines into which deviations can be properly put. A sensitive religious person approaches the deviations of ceremonial forms in a spiritual manner, with a knowledge of their deeper meaning and he has learned to tolerate the various means of physical manipulations. Of course, this means that those in charge of the ceremonial practice must tolerate a deviant in their presence. Toleration and compromise in this context are conditions of fellowship, not the hyprocritical behavior of an insincere person.

Alexander Campbell's program of a non-credal, non-authoritarian framework for Christian unity allows many differing views of experience, religious and philosophical, under the range of one broad heaven. One can believe the creeds if he wishes, but such creeds are not made the test of discipleship; one can entertain almost any doctrine he chooses, but he does not impose this favorite doctrine on another mind. A unity which is gained by the tyranny of one mind over another is not a genuine unity.

Human experience shows that the problems of men are constantly shifting in focus and in significance. When poverty, sickness, and ignorance are uppermost as problems, then the social gospel is relevant. When man feels alone and alienated in a corporate society, then the focus of attention shifts to a new problem. When discrimination, segregation, and racial bigotry are evils to be combatted, then the issue of brotherhood is uppermost. Campbell's broad framework for Christian unity allows its members to face new problems, develop new ideas, even new philosophies and new theologies, without the stigma of heresy.

Is one compelled to accept the particular conclusions of Alexander Campbell's own personal philosophy in order to be a Christian? Certainly not. While he admitted his indebtedness to certain thinkers above all others, to men like Francis Bacon, John Locke, and Dugald Stewart, he did not expect all men to accept his personal philosophy as a final gospel. Campbell did not aspire to have personal followers or to have a revered place in a kind of apostolic succession. Once he remarked that weak minds want to know *who* says something, but strong and vigorous minds never ask this question. The latter ask only if the statement is true. He admitted in his writings that science was in its infancy in the conclusions it makes about the universe, that moral philosophy needed more development, and that scholarship on the Scriptures had only just begun. His was a mind which found delight in searching, and such a mind is undogmatic and open to new experience.

BIBLIOGRAPHY OF ALEXANDER CAMPBELL'S WRITINGS

Compiled by Dr. Claude E. Spencer, curator emeritus, of the Disciples of Christ Historical Society, Nashville, Tennessee. This comprehensive bibliography of Campbell's original writings first appeared in *Disciplina*, Vol. 20, No. 4 and Vol. 20, No. 6, and is used here by permission.

BOOKS

Acts of the Apostles, Translated From the Greek, On the Basis of the Common English Version, With Notes [by Alexander Campbell] New York, American Bible Union, 1857. iv, 224 p.

The Campbell Yearbook, Choice Selections for Every Day in the Year, Compiled by W. G. Burleigh; Biographical Sketch by Peter Ainslie. [Portsmouth, Va., Compiler, 1909] 136 p. front (port.)

Christian Baptism: With its Antecedents and Consequents. Bethany, Va., Printed and Published by Alexander Campbell, 1851. 444 p.

Two different printings were made in 1851. It has been reprinted many times by various publishers; currently by the Gospel Advocate Co., Nashville, Tenn.

The Christian Hymn Book, see Psalms, Hymns, and Spiritual Songs.

The Christian Preacher's Companion; or, the Gospel Facts Sustained by the Testimony of Unbelieving Jews and Pagans. Bethany, Va., [Printed and Published by M'Vay & Ewing] MDCCCXXXVI [156] p.

Also published by A. Campbell, Bethany, Va., 1844, 352 p., under the title: *Infidelity Refuted by Infidels; or, the Gospel Proved by the Testimony of Unbelieving Jews and Pagans;* and reprinted several times by various publishers.

The Christian System, in Reference to the Union of Christians, and a Restoration of Primitive Christianity, as Plead in the Current Reformation. Bethany, Va., Printed by A. Campbell; Pittsburg. Published by Forrester & Campbell, 1839. 368, iv p.

For the first edition of this work see *A Connected View of the Principles...*; reprinted many times by various publishers; currently by the Gospel Advocate, Nashville, Tenn.

A Connected View of the Principles and Rules by Which the Living Oracles May Be Intelligibly and Certainly Interpreted.... Bethany, Va., Printed and Published by M'Vay and Ewing, 1835. 404, iv p.

Cover title: *Christianity Restored*

The first edition of *The Christian System;* Campbell repudiated the cover title as being a binder's error; photolithoprint in 1959 by the Old Paths Book Club, Rosemead, Calif.

A Discussion of the Doctrine of Endless Misery and Universal Salvation, in an Epistolary Correspondence Between Alexander Campbell, of Bethany, Va., and Dolphus Skinner, of Utica, N. Y. Utica, C. C. P. Grosh, Printer, 1840. vi, 7-436 p.

A Debate Between Rev. A. Campbell and Rev. N. L. Rice, on the Action, Subject, Design and Administrator of Christian Baptism ... Held in Lexington, Ky., From the Fifteenth of November to the Second of December, 1843. . . . Lexington, A. T. Skillman & Son; Cincinnati, Wright & Swormstedt, J. A. James; Louisville, D. S. Burnet; New York, R. Carter; Pittsburg, Thomas Carter, 1844. [2] 11-912 p.

Reprinted many times by various publishers; photolithoprint, Old Paths Book Club, Rosemead, Calif., 1956.

A Debate on Christian Baptism, Between the Rev. W. L. MacCalla, a Presbyterian Preacher and Alexander Campell, Held at Washington, Ky. Commencing on the 15th and Terminating on the 21st Oct. 1823. . . . Buffaloe, [Va.], Campbell and Sala, 1824. 420 p.

Reprinted many times by various publishers; photolithoprint issued in 1948 by the Old Paths Book Club.

Debate on Christian Baptism Between Mr. John Walker, a Minister of the Secession and Alexander Campbell, held at Mount-Pleasant on the 19th and 20th June, 1920 ... Second Edition Enlarged. . . . Pittsburg, Published by Eichbaum and Johnston, 1822. [5], 292 p.

For the first edition see *Infant Sprinkling.*

Two photolithoprint editions have been issued; Religious Book Service, Indianapolis, Ind., and Old Paths Book Club, Rosemead, Calif.

Debate on the Evidences of Christianity ... Held in the City of Cincinnati, Ohio, From the 13th to the 21st of April, 1829; Between Robert Owen, of New Lanark, Scotland, and Alexander Campbell, of Bethany, Va. . . . Bethany, Va., Printed and Published by Alexander Campbell, 1829. 2 Vols. in one; Vol. I, 251 p.; Vol. II, 301, [2] p.

Reprinted many times by various publishers; photolithoprint, Gospel Advocate Co., Nashville, Tenn., 1957.

A Debate on the Roman Catholic Religion; Held in the Sycamore Street Meeting House, Cincinnati; From the 13th to the 21st of January, 1837; Between Alexander Campbell and the Rt. Rev. John B. Purcell. . . . Cincinnati, Stereotyped and Published by J. A. James & Co., 1837. viii, 9-359, [1] p.

Reprinted many times by various publishers.

Essays and a Dialogue on the Work of the Holy Spirit in the Salvation of Men. Broekport, N. Y., J. M. Yearnshaw, 1834 ? 70 p.

Reprinted from the *Christian Baptist,* various issues of Vol. 2 and from the *Millennial Harbinger,* Vol. 2.

Familiar Lectures on the Pentateuch; Delivered Before the Morning Class of Bethany College, During the Session of 1859-1860; Also Short Extracts From His Sermons During the Same Session ... ed. With an

Introduction and Occasional Notes by W. T. Moore. Cincinnati, H. S. Bosworth, 1867. 379 p., front. (port.)

Reprinted many times by various publishers; photolithoprint in 1958 by the Old Paths Book Club, Rosemead, Calif.

Infant Sprinkling Proved to be a Human Tradition; Being the Substance of a Debate on Christian Baptism Between Mr. John Walker, a Minister of the Secession and Alexander Campbell, V. D. M., a Regular Baptist Minister, Held at Mount Pleasant, Jefferson County, Ohio, on the 19th and 20th June 1820. Steubenville, O., Printed by James Wilson, 1820. [4], 216 p.

For the second edition, see *Debate on Christian Baptism.*

Infidelity Refuted by Infidels see *The Christian Preacher's Companion.*

Lawrence Greatrake's Calumnies Repell'd. Buffaloe, Brooke Co., Va., Published by A. Campbell, 1825. 60 p.

Letters to a Skeptic. Cincinnati, H. S. Bosworth, 1859. 57 p.

Reprinted from various issues of the *Christian Baptist*, Vol. 4; may have been reprinted as a separate by Campbell in 1826; at least one reprint was made by the Christian Publishing Co., n. d.

The Living Oracles see *The Sacred Writings of the Apostles and Evangelists of Jesus Christ.*

Memoirs of Elder Thomas Campbell Together With a Brief Memoir of Mrs. Jane Campbell. Cincinnati, H. S. Bosworth, 1861. 319 p. front (port.)

Reprinted in 1871; photolithoprint in 1954 by the Old Paths Book Club, Rosemead, Calif.

Popular Lectures and Addresses. Philadelphia, James Challen & Son, 1863. 647 p. front. (port.)

Reprinted many times by various publishers; photolithoprint in 1954 by the Harbinger Book Club, Nashville, Tenn.

Psalms, Hymns and Spiritual Songs. Bethany, Va., A. Campbell, 1828. 192 p.

Four printings were made of the original hymn book.

Psalms, Hymns and Spiritual Songs, Original and Selected, Compiled by A. Campbell, W. Scott, B. W. Stone, and J. T. Johnson; Adapted to the Christian Religon. Bethany, Va., Printed by A. Campbell, 1834. 247, [9] p.

Many printings were made of this revision, the second.

Psalms, Hymns and Spiritual Songs, Original and Selected, Compiled by A. Campbell, W. Scott, B. W. Stone, and J. T. Johnson; Adapted to the Christian Religon. Bethany, Va., Printed and Published by A. Campbell, 1843. 256, 192 p.

Cover title: *The Christian Hymnbook*

Many printings were made of this revision, the third.

Psalms, Hymns and Spiritual Songs, Compiled by A. Campbell, W. Scott, B. W. Stone, and J. T. Johnson, Elders of the Christian Church. With Numerous and Various Additions and Emendations. Adapted to Personal, Family and Church Worship by Alexander Campbell. Bethany, Va., Printed and Published by A. Campbell, 1851. 511 p.

Cover title: *The Christian Hymn Book*

Many printings were made of this revision, the fourth.

The Christian Hymn Book: a Compilation of Psalms, Hymns, and Spiritual Songs, Original and Selected, by A. Campbell and Others. Revised and Enlarged by a Committee. Cincinnati, H. S. Bosworth, 1865. 828 p.

Many printings were made of three different type size of this revision, the fifth and the last to carry Alexander Campbell's name on the title page.

The Sacred Writings of the Apostles and Evangelists of Jesus Christ, Commonly Styled the New Testament. Translated From the Original Greek, by George Campbell, James Macknight, and Philip Doddridge, Doctors of the Church of Scotland. With Prefaces to the Historical and Epistolary Books; and an Appendix, Containing Critical Notes and Various Translations of Difficult Passages. Buffaloe, Brooke county, Virginia. Printed and Published by Alexander Campbell, 1826. 478 [1], xivii p.

Cover title of some printings: *The Living Oracle*

Reprinted several times with revisions by Campbell; reprinted many times by various publishers including Welsh Language editions; photolithoprint by the Harbinger Book Club, Nashville, Tenn., 1951.

Strictures on Three Letters Respecting the Debate at Mount Pleasant [Ohio]; Published in the Presbyterian Magazine in 1821: Signed Samuel Ralston. Pittsburg, Eichbaum and Johnston, 1822. 76 p.

The Writings of Alexander Campbell, Selections Chiefly From the Millennial Harbinger, by W. A. Morris. Austin, Tex., Eugene Von Broeckman, Printer, 1896. xvi, 621 p. front. (port.)

PAMPHLETS

Address Delivered at New Athens College to the Students of That Institution by Special Request of Students and Faculty, at Annual Commencement. Published by the Students, 1838.

Printed in *The Millennial Harbinger*, November, 1838.

An Address Delivered Before the Charlottesville [Va.] Lyceum, on the 16th of June, 1840 [sic]. Published at the Request of the Lyceum. 22 p.

Printed in *The Millennial Harbinger*, August, 1841; reprinted in his *Popular Lectures and Addresses*, 1863.

An Address Delivered to the Members of the Jefferson Literary Society of Franklin College, New Athens, Ohio, September 25, 1838. Bethany, Va., Printed by A. Campbell, 1838. 23 p.

67632

An Address Delivered to the Young Men's Mercantile Library Association of Cincinnati; on the Anglo-Saxon Language, Its Origin, Character and Destiny, Dec. 11, 1849. . . . Bethany, Va., 1850. 34 p.

Printed in *The Millennial Harbinger*, May, 1850; reprinted in his *Popular Lectures and Addresses*, 1863; original manuscript in the archives of the Disciples of Christ Historical Society.

An Address on Capital Punishment, Delivered to the Washington Literary Institute, on the Evening of March 2d, 1846, Published by Request. Bethany, Va., Printed by A. Campbell, 1846. 34 p.

Printed in *The Millennial Harbinger*, March, 1846; reprinted in his *Popular Lectures and Addresses*, 1863.

An Address on Demonology, Delivered Before the Popular Lecture Club, Nashville, Tenn., March 10, 1841.

No copy known of the first edition; printed in *The Millennial Harbinger*, October, 1841; reprinted by Charles G. Berry, 1851; reprinted in his *Popular Lectures and Addresses*, 1863.

An Address on the Amelioration of the Social State, Delivered . . . Louisville. Louisville, Prentice and Weissinger, 1839. 31 p.

Reprinted in *The Millennial Harbinger*, July, 1840; reprinted in his *Popular Lectures and Addresses*, 1863.

An Address on War; Delivered Before the Wheeling Lyceum, May 11th, 1848. [Bethany, Va. ? Printed by A. Campbell ?, 1848 ?]. 24 p.

Printed in *The Millennial Harbinger*, July, 1848; reprinted in his *Popular Lectures and Addresses*, 1863; reprinted in the *Congressional Record* November 22, 1937, and issued as a 19 page separate.

An Address to the Members of the Union Literary Society, of Miami University, Ohio. Bethany, Va., Printed by A. Campbell, 1844. 23 p. Caption title: *Responsibilities of Men of Genius. . . .*

Printed in *The Millennial Harbinger*, December, 1844; reprinted in his *Popular Lectures and Addresses*, 1863.

Alexander Campbell on the Book of Mormon, see *Mormonism. . .*

Baccalaureate Address, Delivered to Ten Graduates at Bethany College, July 4th, 1845. Bethany, Va., Printed by A. Campbell, 1845, 12 p.

Printed in *The Millennial Harbinger*, July, 1845.

Breaking the Loaf see Periodicals — *The Millennial Harbinger Extra,* no. 2.

Character of "The Debate on Campbellism," see Periodicals — *The Millennial Harbinger Extra,* no. 5.

A Circular Letter Written by Mr. Alexander Campbell at the Request of the Redstone Baptist Association to the Churches in Their Connexion . . . Setember 4, 1817. [n. p.] 1817.

Reprinted as *Views of Mr. Alexander Campbell Concerning the Doctrines of Election and Reprobation.* Fulton, Mo., T. L. Stephens, 1856, 22 p.

Delusions see *Mormonism.* . . .

Education see Periodicals — *The Millennial Harbinger Extra,* no. 9.

Extra Defended; Being an Examination of Mr. A. Broadus "Extra Examined" see Periodicals — *The Millennial Harbinger Extra,* no. 3.

Facts and Documents Confirmatory of the Credibility of the Debate on Baptism, Between W. L. M'Calla and Alexander Campbell, Being a Full Exposition of a "Unitarian Baptist" Created and Made by the Rev. W. L. M'Calla. Bethany, Brooke Co., Va. [A. Campbell], 1828. 24 p.

Kingdom of Heaven see Periodicals — *The Millennial Harbinger Extra,* no. 7.

Life and Death. Cincinnati, H. S. Bosworth, 1860. 96 p.

Reprint of an "Extra" of *The Millennial Harbinger,* unnumbered but dated December, 1844; reprinted in his *Popular Lectures and Addresses,* 1863; reprinted various times under various imprints.

Life and Death see also Periodicals — *The Millennial Harbinger Extra,* no. 12.

Lecture on Slavery, Delivered Within the Waterloo Room, Edinburgh, on Friday, August 13, 1847. Edinburgh, R. M. Walker, [1847]. 16 p.

Reprinted from the Edinburgh *Journal,* 18th August, 1847.

The Lunenburg Letter With Attendant Comments. Nashville, Tenn., Disciples of Christ Historical Society, 1953. [16] p. (Footnotes to Disciple History, no. 2)

Reprinted from *The Millennial Harbinger,* September, November and December, 1837.

The Memorable Sermon on the Law see *The Substance of a Sermon.* . . .

Mormonism. The Book of Mormon Reviewed, and its Divine Pretensions Exposed. Delusions. Bethany, Va., [Printed by A. Campbell ?, 1831 ?] 12 p.

Probably reprinted from *The Millennial Harbinger* of February 7, 1831; reprints have been made under the title Delusions, 1832 and 1925, and *Alexander Campbell on the Book of Mormon,* 1902?

On Moral Societies. [New York], The International Religious Liberty Association, 1898. 24 p. (Religious Liberty Library, No. 53, extra, May, 1898.)

"The Candidus Papers," reprinted from the Washington, Pa., *Reporter,* 1820.

Order see Periodicals — *The Millennial Harbinger Extra,* no. 9.

Order of Worship, Compiled by C. M. Stubblefield. Cincinnati, F. L. Rowe, 1915. 31 p.

Reprinted from Vol. 2 of the *Christian Baptist.*

The Philosophy of Memory and of Commemorative Institutions: an Address, Delivered by Request to the "Union Literary Society," of Washington College, November 10th, 1841. Bethany, Va., Printed by A. Campbell, 1841. 23 p.

Printed in *The Millennial Harbinger*, December, 1841; reprinted in his *Popular Lectures and Addresses*, 1863.

The Rank and Dignity of Man; an Address Delivered to the Students of Florence Academy, Washington County, Pennsylvania (at their request) Bethany, Va., Printed by A. Campbell, 1838. 23 p.

Printed in *The Millennial Harbinger*, December, 1838.

Regeneration see Periodicals — *The Millennial Harbinger Extra*, no. 6.

Remission of Sins. [Titusville, Pa., H. R. Press, 1949] 108 p.

Reprint of an "Extra" of *The Millennial Harbinger*, dated July 5, 1830. *Remission of Sins* see also Periodicals — *The Millennial Harbinger Extra*, no. 1.

Report of the Proceedings of a General Meeting of Messengers, From Thirteen Congregations, Held in Wellsburg, Va., On Saturday, the 12th of April, 1834, by J. T. M'Vay and A. Campbell. [Bethany, Va.?, A. Campbell?, 1834?] 12 p.

Reprinted, 1957, by the Disciples of Christ Historical Society, Nashville, Tenn., as *Footnotes to Disciple History*, no. 5.

A Review of a Review of Something Called "Campbellism" see Periodicals — *The Millennial Harbinger Extra*, no. 11.

Schism; its Bane and Antidote, or the True Foundation of Christian Union. London, Simpkin & Co.; Nottingham, R. Groombridge and T. Kirk, 1840. 30 p.

A second edition was published in London, 1846, under the title: *The True Foundation of Christian Union: Shewing the Practicability of the Union and Communion of All God's People.*

Sermon on the Law see *The Substance of a Sermon.*

The Substance of a Sermon Delivered Before the Redstone Baptist Association, Met on Cross Creek, Brooke County, Va., on the First of September 1816. . . . Steubenville, O., James Wilcox, 1816. 35 p.

Reprinted under the title: *The Memorable Sermon on the Law*, St. Louis, Christian Publishing Co., 1889. 51 p.; reprinted in *Historical Documents Advocating Christian Union*, ed. by A. C. Young, Chicago, 1904.

Supernatural Facts: an Address Delivered to the Maysville Lyceum, March 25th, 1839. Published by Request of the Institution. Bethany, Va., Printed by A. Campbell, 1839. 24 p.

Reprinted from *The Millennial Harbinger*, June, 1839; reprinted in his *Popular Lectures and Addresses*, 1863.

A Tract for the People of Kentucky. [Louisville, Courier Office, 1849?] 8 p.

The True Foundation of Christian Union see *Schism; its Bane and Antidote.*

Views of Mr. Alexander Campbell Concerning the Doctrines of Election and Reprobation see *A Circular Letter.*

PERIODICALS

The Christian Baptist, Buffaloe Creek and Bethany, Va., published monthly from August, 1823 through July, 1830. 7 Vols., with A. Campbell as the editor.

Early issues were reprinted by Campbell; reprinted [not a photo-lithoprint] by the Gospel Advocate Co., Nashville, Tenn., 1955-1956.

The Christian Baptist, edited by Alexander Campbell, revised by D. S. Burnet, from the Second Edition, with Mr. Campbell's Last Corrections, Seven Volumes in One. Cincinnati, Published by D. S. Burnet, 1835. vi [2], 670 p.

Reprinted many times by different publishers.

The Millennial Harbinger, Bethany, Va., published monthly from January, 1830 through 1863, 34 vols., with A. Campbell as the editor. The periodical continued through 1870 with W. K. Pendleton as editor, 7 vols.

Photolithoprints of the first ten years have been issued by the Harbinger Book Club, Nashville, Tenn., and the Old Paths Book Club, Rosemead, Calif.

The Millennial Harbinger Abridged, by Benjamin Lyon Smith, Intro-duction by Charles Louis Loos. Cincinnati, Standard Publishing Co., 1902. 2 vols., 588, 690 p. "Includes index to the forty [sic] volumes of *The Millennial Harbinger*," and of *The Millennial Harbinger Abridged.*

The Millennial Harbinger, Extra:

No. [1],   July 5, 1830. *Remission of Sins.* 60 p.

2 ,   December, 1830. *Breaking the Loaf.* 61-88 p.

3 ,   October 10, 1831. *Extra Defended; Being an Examination of Mr. A. Broadus "Extra Examined."* 48 p.

4 ,   August 6, 1832. *[Questions and Answers.]* 337-372 p.

5 ,   August 6, 1832. *Character of "The Debate on Campbellism,"* by Obadiah Jennings, D.D. 421-432 p.

6 ,   August 5, 1833. *Regeneration.* 337-384 p.

7 ,   August, 1834. *Kingdom of Heaven.* 385-444 p.

8 ,   October, 1835. *Order.* 481-528 p.

9 ,   December, 1836. *Education.* 577-608 p.

[10],   December, 1837. *Extra No. 1 New Series* [Deals with the John Thomas Controversy]. 577-588 p.

11 ,   October, 1839. *A Review of a Review of Something Called "Campbellism."* 481-504 p.

[12],   December, 1844. *Life and Death.* 529-574 p.

[13],   [April, 1847]. *Bethany College.* 8 p.

INDEX